"You are the parent. If you can change and do what this wonderful book invites you to change and do, then you can give the most precious gift to your child—transforming your child's "problem" into a strength. Please accept the gift of this book—for your child's sake."

—*Alvin R. Mahrer, Ph.D., professor emeritus of psychology*

a   ie
C

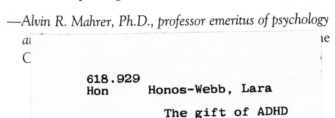
"Honos-Wel   it with this enlighte   jumped to sections   "Why Medications   ed and enlightening   d a lot. You will too

—T
G   tic
P

"Honos-   their parents,   her message   and even the   for anyone v   this diagnosis   find a radical   heir own gifts

the **Gift** of ADHD

How to Transform Your Child's Problems into Strengths

LARA HONOS-WEBB, PH.D.

New Harbinger Publications, Inc.

Copyright © 2005 by Lara Honos-Webb
New Harbinger Publications, Inc.
5674 Shattuck Avenue
Oakland, CA 94609

Cover design by Amy Shoup
Acquired by Tesilya Hanauer
Edited by Carole Honeychurch
Text design by Tracy Marie Carlson

ISBN 1-57224-389-9 Paperback
Distributed in Canada by Raincoast Books
All Rights Reserved
Printed in the United States of America

New Harbinger Publications' Web site address: www.newharbinger.com

07   06   05

10   9   8   7   6   5   4   3   2

Contents

Acknowledgments

I gratefully dedicate this book to Ken and Kenny Webb for making me happy and making me laugh through all the hard work that writing this book required.

I thank my brother, John Honos, and my mother, Karen Honos, for giving me a front-row seat to understanding ADHD as a gift. John's unique gifts are the inspiration for this book. Thanks also to Edward, Chrissty, and Grace Honos for being my cheerleaders along the way. I also appreciate the support from and interesting conversations with Carole, Bill, and Lynn Webb and Anna and Dale Chalfant.

This book is greatly indebted to the scholarly work of Larry Leitner, whose pioneering work on humanistic assessment is the primary scholarly inspiration for the approach taken in the book. Also, if he hadn't read my presentation in Toronto, this book would never have been. I am grateful for his generosity as a mentor and friend. I'm also grateful for the support of members of Division 32. Special thanks to Marc Celentana, Timothy Anderson, April Faidley, Art Bohart, Constance Fischer, Kathleen Wall, Olga Louchakova, Tom Greening, and Al Mahrer.

I also want to thank my acquisitions editor, Tesilya Hanauer, for her incredible support throughout the process and for her initial interest in my work. Thank you for seeing so much potential in my views on ADHD and my work. I am also grateful for the editorial work of Heather Mitchener and for the lovely conversation she and her husband Kris provided over Turkish food. Thanks also to Carole Honeychurch for her thorough editorial assistance.

So much of the book was shaped by stimulating conversations with colleagues Cy Estonactac, Jenny Yeaggy, Rose Pacini, and Jeannie Lopez. Thanks to Kimberly McCoy for her special insights and sharing of personal experiences. Thanks to Michael Axelman and Sue Parry for helpful conversations and resources as I was writing this book. Thanks to Pedro Hernandez-Ramos for the conversation that led to the metaphor of ADHD children as canaries in the coal mine and the references to scholarship in technology and education. Thanks also to Father Sonny Manuel for the course scheduling that allowed me the time to write the book in such a short time.

I thank all of my students, with a special thanks to Lee Ann O'Neal and Jeni Johnstone for personal stories of parenting children with the gift of ADHD. I thank Amy Williams for sharing her clinical experiences. Thanks to Kimberly Krochock and Gina Biegel for helping me track down relevant journal articles. I am grateful to William Cangemi and Elizabeth Harrick for their original interest in the research project that led to this book.

Last but not least, many thanks to those who supported me with child care and emotional support while writing the book. Thanks to Theresa Lopes, Elizabeth Soares, Andreia Drumm, and Nancy O'Brien for their loving care of Kenny. Thanks to Carolynn Kohn, Renie Oxley, Laura Ellingson, Lisa, Peter, and Rochelle Cloven, Margareth and Victoria Click, Wendy and Colton Whittles, Bettina and Max Hayak, Lane Arye and A Diamond for your warm support.

Introduction

Why has the diagnosis of attention-deficit/hyperactivity disorder (ADHD) received so much attention recently? One can hardly watch a television show or read a popular magazine without seeing an advertisement for a new and improved medication for treating children diagnosed with this disorder. With all the media attention this disorder has received in the popular press recently, the label ADHD has taken on a power of its own. Media outlets would have us believe that ADHD has grown to epidemic proportions. Researchers estimate that from 3 to 5 percent of all school-aged children have been given the diagnosis of ADHD (American Psychiatric Association 2000). ADHD is three times more likely in boys than in girls (Barkley 2000). Estimates indicate that the rates of diagnosis of ADHD have increased 400 percent since 1988 (Stein 1999), though the explosion of this disorder seems confined to the United States. For every two hundred and fifty children diagnosed and treated with ADHD, only one child would similarly have been diagnosed and treated in all of Germany, England, France, and Italy combined (Furman 2002). In addition to accounts of increasing rates of prevalence, the label has come to take on the sense of being almost an insult. As a parent of a child with ADHD, you may find comfort that you are not alone facing the recent explosion of information, services, and medications aimed at treating ADHD. You may also feel confused by so much information, much of it contradictory.

WHAT IS ADHD?

ADHD is often used in an offhand manner to describe children who seem to be out of control. Actually, it is a diagnosis that requires that many specific criteria be met. The two major dimensions of ADHD according to the *Diagnostic and Statistical Manual of Mental Disorders* (American Psychiatric Association 2000) are inattention and hyperactivity/impulsivity.

The behavioral symptoms of inattention include making careless mistakes, being easily distracted, and having a difficult time completing projects. Other behavioral manifestations of inattention include difficulty listening, difficulty following directions, and difficulty with organization, often losing homework and other things, and being late or forgetting appointments.

The symptoms of the hyperactivity dimension include fidgeting, difficulty in sitting still, excessive talking, and difficulty with quiet activities. Children often feel as if they are being driven by a motor. Impulsive symptoms include blurting out inappropriate comments, an inability to wait one's turn, and acting without thinking.

While many children display some of these symptoms some of the time, a diagnosis of ADHD requires that there be evidence that these symptoms are severe enough to impair functioning in more than one setting. Usually this means that the child has to be disruptive both in a school setting and at home. Furthermore, a diagnosis of ADHD requires that other possible disorders be ruled out. For example, a child who is anxious, depressed, or oppositional may have many symptoms that look like ADHD. However, if the symptoms are better explained by another diagnosis, ADHD would not be given as a diagnosis.

This brief overview clarifies that a diagnosis of ADHD requires a thorough assessment and usually entails getting information from children, parents, and teachers. Because the diagnosis requires evidence that the behavioral disruptions occur in more than one setting, teachers and parents play an important role in a formal assessment process.

If your child has been given a diagnosis of ADHD without a very thorough assessment that involved testing and checklists for parents and teachers, you may want to consider a second opinion. Because the diagnosis may impact your child's expectations and self-worth, you want to be sure that a thorough evaluation has been conducted by a trained professional.

WHO THIS BOOK IS FOR, AND HOW IT'S DIFFERENT

This book is intended for parents of children who are six to twelve years old and have been diagnosed with ADHD by a trained professional, parents who are interested in transforming not only their child's symptoms, but their own vision of what ADHD means. As described in the next section, this book will make a case that ADHD is a gift. Even if you found yourself relieved that your child was diagnosed with ADHD because it finally seemed to offer an answer to many of your questions about your child's behavior, this book will be helpful to you. Even if you are glad that your child has a diagnosis, this book can help, because it agrees that what gets diagnosed as ADHD is a very real difference. Your child is different from other children in predictable ways. This book will help you to see that while your child's differences pose many challenges, they also offer many gifts. So whether you were happy, relieved, distressed, or distraught when your child was diagnosed with ADHD, this book will guide you to help transform your vision of your child and your relationship with your child and his symptoms.

This book is also different because it recognizes that the treatment plan has to match the difference that your child exhibits. Many books for helping children and parents with ADHD offer very complicated, labor-intensive exercises for parents and children to do. These are not so helpful because children, and sometimes parents, have difficulty completing and following through with lengthy, complicated forms and long, drawn-out exercises.

The techniques in the book are designed to cater to your child's differences. They will use his gift for wanting concrete sensory engagement rather than abstract theorizing as a strategy for learning new information. Also, many of the exercises ask you to build on areas of specialized interest that your child already has a lot of energy for, whether it's Harry Potter or Barry Bonds. You will help your child channel his existing energy for special interests into pretend games that transform his symptoms.

As you go through the book, it will be important to remember that there are more than enough exercises throughout to help transform your child's problems into strengths. If you or your child don't like some of the exercises, don't push it. Just move on to another exercise. The best strategy will be to find a handful of the exercises that your child enjoys so much that it feels like you and he are playing and to use those exercises over time. You can think of these as like going to the gym to build muscles. The more he learns how to manage his thoughts, behaviors, and sense of self-worth, the more powerfully you'll see him transform. You will also find that these exercises are not just another thing to do that pits you and your child against each other. Rather, they will be fun things for you and your child to share in and to build your relationship and closeness with each other.

ADHD AS A GIFT: A PARADIGM SHIFT

This book will offer you not just another piece of information, but rather a radically new way of looking at your child's diagnosis. This book suggests that while (as you well know) your child is different, the constellation of traits labeled as ADHD is in fact a gift. This book offers you a "paradigm shift" in how you understand your child. A *paradigm* shift is a change in the way we see things. To go from seeing your child as having a deficit disorder to seeing your child as having a unique gift would be a major shift that would help both you and your child. This radical way of revisioning your child and his differences will be the starting point for developing a program of change that will help you shift from being your child's apologist to being your child's advocate. As an apologist for your child, you may have accepted the critical comments of his teachers and felt apologetic about his behavior. As an advocate for your child, you will learn to gently challenge the teacher's criticism and reframe your child's behavior in a more positive light, providing the teacher with helpful suggestions for handling your child's differences.

At first you may greet the positive reframing of ADHD as welcome news but also find it difficult to believe because perhaps your child's teachers, pediatrician, and psychiatrist have all told you that your child has a serious problem. It can be very difficult to even consider that all these experts might be wrong. You may have even found yourself frustrated with your child's behavior and lack of motivation and perhaps feeling relieved to know that there is a name for your child's problems.

The many educators and health professionals you have encountered are not necessarily wrong; your child is indeed different and in a way that our culture has not learned to fully appreciate. In our culture, differences almost always get defined as a disorder. So these care providers are right in their judgment that your child is different from other children. They are also correct in another sense—your child's behavior may have become problematic in ways that are not related to the gifts of ADHD. But educators and health-care providers may have failed to notice the ways in which the diagnosis of ADHD itself can cause problems in behavior, attention, and motivation.

So the people who have given this diagnosis to your child are right that your child is different and correct in their observations that some problematic behaviors have emerged. Where they may not be entirely right is in seeing these differences as problems to be corrected rather than potential gifts and opportunities. This book will help reveal the ways in which your child's gifts have a lot to offer, both to himself and to the world.

My first encounter with ADHD came about at a young age, when my own brother was diagnosed with this disorder long before it was a popular diagnosis. In fact, when he was diagnosed, most people hadn't even heard of ADHD. While he was given medication to help manage his behavior in the classroom, my mother never understood it as a disorder. She regaled us with stories about how intuitive my brother was and how sensitive he was to her and other people's emotions. We all noticed it. As a family, we saw that while he often burst out with irreverent comments to and about the people we encountered, he was amazingly perceptive. When my mother reluctantly agreed to put him on medication, she viewed it as a concession to particular teachers who could not manage my brother in the classroom. She also found that whether he took medication or not depended on the teacher. Some years he would need the medication, but with some teachers he did well and wouldn't need medication at school. It was my mother's understanding that medication was a means of appeasing others. For example, she would give my brother his medication when her own mother came to visit. My grandmother had no ability to tolerate my brother's rambunctious behavior, and so my mom would give the medication to my brother so my grandmother would not get so disturbed.

As a clinical psychologist I have spent years training to be sensitive to other people's emotions and to understand interpersonal interactions. In spite of all my training, I have found that my brother's ability to capture the complexities of interpersonal interactions and other people's emotional states far surpasses my own—and almost any of my well-trained colleagues. I came to understand that he possessed an interpersonal intuition that no amount of training could bestow. Psychologists spend a lot of time learning how to read a person beyond what they say about who they are. Children with ADHD have a keen ability to see the insincerity in people and not be fooled by a person's efforts to appear to be something they are not. While this represents a gift of interpersonal intuition, you can see that without some training in how to use this gift, it can create problems in relationships for your ADHD child, who may be prone to making irreverent comments based on his perceptions.

The Frustration of Being Misunderstood

The following is a typical example of what happens to children with ADHD in treatment settings. Jack was a patient on a child and adolescent psychiatric unit. One day, as he was sitting in a session of group therapy, Jack noticed that the nurse running the session had a seemingly permanent sour expression and was treating the young group members with disdain. She displayed little compassion for the struggles the patients faced, coming from disturbed families and diagnosed with mental illnesses at such an early age.

Jack, who had been given the diagnosis of ADHD, was making faces at her—in some way mirroring her sour expression but amplifying it. His behavior was appropriate for a seven-year-old boy. Although he was somewhat impulsive in his display, he created a very astute characterization of the nurse. Unfortunately, the nurse overreacted, threatening the boy with severe punishment if he didn't stop making faces at her. As she escalated her threats, his mocking behavior escalated to the point where two large, male staff members intervened, putting Jack in isolation and one-to-one watch for the rest of the day.

When Jack was carried out, his behavior had escalated to the point where he did in fact look like an immensely disturbed child. He thrashed his body around as he was carried out, screaming loudly about the injustice of the way he was being treated. However, the blame could also be pointed at the nurse, whose behavior was unprofessional. It's easy to understand why a small child who is emotionally sensitive and interpersonally astute would become angry and disturbed in this situation. The nurse displayed a lack of sensitivity to him, given his age and level of emotional maturity. However, in part because of his diagnosis, the setting of an inpatient hospital, and the nurse's own disposition, the situation escalated through a vicious cycle, creating behavioral excesses that seemed to prove how disturbed the boy was.

In another setting, one for example that was not aimed at controlling the boy, he might have been able to express his exuberance, interpersonal intuition (as demonstrated in his capacity to capture and reflect back to the nurse her own sour expression), and intense emotional sensitivity. Instead, the nurse's increasingly punitive stance impacted him deeply, aggravating his predisposition toward uncontrolled behavior.

As a teacher and clinical psychologist, I've found that my observations about my brother also applied to other individuals who had been given the diagnosis of ADHD. As a teacher, I found that the students who had been given this diagnosis were often the most engaging interpersonally and also the most intellectually creative. While it was true that the students with ADHD often received the lowest grades in the courses I taught, they far surpassed their peers in their ability to engage the material in creative ways. They were often stimulated by what they were learning, but not interested in mastering it in the ways standard educational testing assesses. I often found that students with ADHD were the most stimulating to talk with about classroom material because they often made me think in ways I'd never considered before. In contrast, the students who got As seemed most interested in getting good grades and getting the "right" answer. The students with ADHD were interested in forging their own understandings and pushing the limits of what was known by asking new questions, rather than settling for the accepted answers.

GIFT OR DISORDER?

You have likely noted these very same gifts in your child, but you may have felt steamrolled by the choir of voices insisting that these very same traits are symptoms of disturbance. You may also have struggled with the fact that your child really is quite a handful. Children with this diagnosis are a lot of work, and they do act in problematic ways that disrupt others. This book will acknowledge both sides of this reality—the gift and the disruption it causes to others. It's important to keep in mind that any difference will be disruptive to others. For example, intellectually precocious children who haven't been diagnosed with ADHD also can be disruptive in traditional educational settings, because they get bored and can act out, distracting other students struggling with the material that is so simple for the gifted child. So, while it's true that your child may be "a problem" for his teacher, it's also a fact that any child with significant differences represents a problem. However, this book will help show you how to understand your child's differences as a gift and change any of his behavior that hinders him. At the same time, let's acknowledge the very real difficulties you and your child will face in a culture that still sees your child as disordered.

CHANGING PROBLEMATIC BEHAVIORS

So in addition to trying to provide a balance between the vision of ADHD as a gift and the reality of the difficulties in managing your child's behavior and the system he interacts with, I will also present a balance between shifting your vision and offering concrete exercises for changing problematic expressions of your child's behavior. This may seem like a contradiction. You may wonder, "On the one hand, it seems like you're saying that my child is gifted, and on the other hand, it seems like you are telling me how to change my child." Both of these things are needed for many reasons.

Even though your child is gifted, the label of ADHD can have a negative impact, which can lead to problematic behaviors. For example, if your son thinks he is stupid, he will have a hard time being highly motivated in school. If children with ADHD believe that they will fail, they will avoid trying so as to be able to protect their self-esteem. It is easier to say, "I didn't try" than to say, "I tried and failed." The label that tells them they have a deficit and a disorder also tells them that they are not equal to others, and this often leads to lack of motivation. As a result of their differences and the challenges of being diagnosed as disordered, your child has adopted coping strategies that are in fact problematic. This book will offer strategies for changing these coping strategies that are failing your child.

Another reason your child may need to alter some behaviors is that the school systems and health-care systems have not yet recognized that your child's differences are a gift. This failure has probably led to negative interaction cycles between your child and professionals in these fields that can create problematic behavior in your child. For example, school settings and treatment settings are often profoundly invalidating to your child. And your child is likely to have the ability to detect when he is being negated or undervalued and to have strong emotional reactions. He sees clearly how he is being dismissed and feels intensely hurt and humiliated by these interactions.

These intense feelings combined with impulsiveness often lead to episodes of acting out that, when escalated by intolerant teachers and professionals, tend to be perceived as profoundly disturbed behavior. When this dynamic is repeated, your child will probably develop coping strategies that may appear to be ingrained behavioral problems. These behaviors need to be changed so that others don't make negative judgments against your child, causing even more upset and disruptive behavior, which continues the pattern of escalating problematic behavior. Because of these tensions, this book will be balanced between changing your vision of your child, helping you change your child's vision of himself, and offering specific exercises for changing and managing behaviors that have become problematic.

POWERFUL OR POWERLESS

As a parent, you have an enormous amount of power to heal your child. You may feel powerless in your interactions with the educational system and the health-care system, but there is much you can do to help your child. The school and health settings may not have conveyed this message to you, and yet it's true.

You may have felt angry with these systems for conveying such disempowering messages to you. You may have heard that your child is profoundly disturbed, that his brain is dysfunctional, that you must have done something wrong or are continuing to do something wrong. All of these communications to you are not necessarily true and can be defeating to you and your child. This book will help you reclaim your power in relation to yourself, your child, the school systems, and your health-care providers.

When you heard a seemingly hopeless diagnosis and the misguided notions about your child from people who were in positions of authority, you may have felt more powerless, assuming that they knew better than you about your child's condition. While you may not be a psychologist or teacher, the paradigm shift described in this book may be in line with your own inner voice that told you the negative descriptions of your child just weren't right. While you may have struggled with your child yourself, perhaps you've found yourself resisting the severity of the diagnosis of ADHD, which may have felt more like an insult than a medical term.

The Gift of ADHD offers information to help you to connect with your own feelings that your child may not be as "all bad" as some of the authorities have told you. You have the power to reclaim your own belief in your child's abilities, strengths, and gifts. It's not that the health-care providers are bad people or are deliberately misleading you—they themselves have been misled by applying a medical model to psychological problems.

Your own expectations for your child will provide a powerful influence. So if you can trust your own positive feelings about your child's strengths, amplify those feelings, and communicate them clearly to your child, you can powerfully impact your child for the better. Your own perceptions of your child's gifts may have become a "still, small voice" (1 Kings 19:12) by now as other authorities have drowned out your own reactions to your child's exuberance, surplus of energy, and emotional sensitivity. This book will support you in reconnecting with your own delight in your child's differences.

Chapter Summaries

The first four chapters of the book will review the paradigm shift represented in the vision of this book—that ADHD is a gift. Chapter 1 will review current understandings of the diagnosis as a disorder and review a countertrend in psychology that argues that differences are not disorders. In line with this paradigm shift, chapter 2 will introduce you to the cognitive behavioral approach to transforming your child. Specific strategies for strengthening your bond to your child will be offered. Chapter 3 will suggest that this sweeping revision of this diagnostic label can also have the therapeutic effect of raising your child's self-esteem. This chapter will also review how self-esteem can be lowered by the diagnosis of ADHD and how each symptom of the disorder, such as impulsiveness, lack of motivation, and lack of attention can also be seen as resulting from lowered self-esteem, not from the purported brain differences alleged to cause ADHD. Chapter 4 will encourage and support you in shifting both your vision and your behavior as you become an advocate for your child rather than his apologist.

In chapters 5 through 9 we will review the specific nature of your child's gifts. In chapter 5 we will review the ways in which children who have been diagnosed with ADHD are creative. We will see, for example, how goofing off is a necessary requirement for creativity. In chapter 6, we will review how your child is particularly gifted with an ecological consciousness—this means an attunement with the natural world. We will also consider the more radical idea that, given the current destruction of the environment, ADHD children can act as guides or "way-showers" with a connection to the natural world that may be what the world needs to save itself. In chapter 7, we will review the interpersonal intuition common in children diagnosed with ADHD. In chapter 8, we will review the ways in which hyperactivity can be viewed as a surplus of energy, as a form of exuberance to be tapped into rather than managed away. In this chapter, specific strategies will be offered for channeling this energy in ways that do not disrupt others. In chapter 9, we'll discuss the ways in which ADHD children are emotionally sensitive and expressive. The balance between appreciating the gift and managing the lack of control it can bring will be addressed with specific strategies. The final chapter will review strategies for navigating both educational and mental-health treatment systems. As you can see, *The Gift of ADHD* will offer you practical suggestions and strategies that accommodate both your inner voice that has appreciated your child's differences and the one that has grown impatient with his behavior and frustrated with the knowledge that his behavior can be a problem for others.

CHAPTER I

Difference Is Not a Disorder or a Deficit

Different historical epochs seem characterized by popular diagnoses. ADHD would be a likely candidate for a diagnosis that characterizes our society at this point in history. According to the *Diagnostic and Statistical Manual of Mental Disorders*, symptoms of ADHD include difficulty paying attention, impulsivity, and hyperactivity (American Psychiatric Association 2000). However, clinical anecdote suggests that individuals diagnosed with ADHD also tend to be particularly insightful, imaginative, and intuitive.

As a parent of a child with this diagnosis you are probably quite familiar with the symptoms it's associated with. As we examined in the introduction, children have difficulty controlling their behavior, act out in impulsive ways, disrupt classes and other students, and find it almost impossible to focus on academic tasks. Lack of concentration leads to poor discipline, impaired relationships due to an inability to listen to others, and difficulty maintaining a routine.

Recent debates on ADHD reveal two dominant positions. One is that ADHD is a brain disorder, and the other is that individuals with this diagnosis are not really different from others, but that our culture does not tolerate rambunctious children. This book takes a position that is different from both of these arguments.

ONE OF THESE KIDS IS NOT LIKE THE OTHERS

There is something about ADHD children that is noticeably different from children who have not been given this diagnosis. This book asserts that to call this difference a disorder is an interpretation—one that has negative effects on your child.

The name of the diagnosis itself shows how medical terminology can be subjective and tends to pathologize a person in a no-win fashion. For example, children with ADHD have *hyperactivity*, which means too much activity. Why are normal children not considered to have an "activity deficit" or "hypoactivity disorder"? But to add insult to injury, ADHD children also have an "attention deficit." Again, one might ask why other children are not considered to have "hyperattention disorder" or an "overfocusing condition." This is meant to illustrate that you should not be too discouraged by the medicalization of the description of your child. Differences do *not* mean disorders, and it is an interpretative leap to say that they do. Differences could be just that—no better or worse, just different from others. Many say "vive la difference!" or that variety is the spice of life. Psychiatrists do not say that. They are trained to see differences as disorders. If one were to apply the logic of seeing differences as disorders to gender, the medical profession might well label women with a "penis-deficit/hypermammary disorder."

Differences may also indicate that someone has a gift or is in some way better than others who don't have the difference. The basis of evolution and natural selection is mutation, or difference. As a species, we have evolved through differences that are found to be adaptive. Many differences give people advantages. Also, in our culture today, we advance in leaps and bounds through creativity—

the ability to think differently from others. In earlier times, a person's career depended on the ability to follow a specific set of instructions, to follow through on instructions from authority. It can be argued that in today's technological culture, a person is more likely to get ahead by coming up with different ways of seeing the world rather than by conforming to authority.

In this book, I will argue not only that ADHD is a difference, but that it is a gift. It confers advantages to the child that have not fully begun to be appreciated. One way in which ADHD children are different is that they are more engaged with the organic world in a sensuous way. They have more difficulty with abstract book knowledge, but have a love of nature, animals, and the human body in a direct, engaged way. In these days of environmental destruction and rampant pollution, these kids seem to demonstrate a form of ecological consciousness that some have argued is necessary to save the planet.

Whether or not you believe that the environment is in danger or even that this is an important cause, this illustration does point to the potential that a difference may be adaptive. Many times differences evolve to solve problems that are caused by the "normal" way of doing things. The perspective of this book is that children with ADHD have a different way of doing things that will solve problems that cannot be solved by doing things in the normal way.

A DISORDER OF THE BRAIN?

The perspective of this book is greatly at odds with current understandings of ADHD. The main difference is that your child's mental-health treatment provider, pediatrician, and teacher understand ADHD as first, a disorder, and second, a medical dysfunction related to *brain pathology* (a dysfunction or disease of the brain). Current explanations highlight the importance of *neuropsychological deficits* (a psychological problem attributed to faulty brain functioning) and brain anomalies. According to one account, "Although ADHD is a biological disorder, the lesion or lesions producing it have yet to be identified. Some studies have implicated the orbital-frontal region, the limbic pathways, and especially the striatium" (Kane et al. 1990, 628). As a neuropsychiatric disorder, current methods of assessment often include brain imaging. Treatment providers have found that the use of such brain-imaging methods promotes compliance with medication to treat ADHD by offering a plausible explanation for problematic behavior.

Sophisticated brain-imaging techniques have seemingly con-firmed that ADHD is a disorder by demonstrating brain differences in children with ADHD. However, brain imaging is not an unimpeach-able, unquestionable authority. You should not be bowled over by the seemingly irrefutable nature of the sophisticated technologies of science. These brain-imaging findings indicate differences, not neces-sarily disorders. For example, sophisticated brain-imaging techniques have found that individuals who are in love show demonstrable differences in brain structure and function. Yet few would label falling in love as a psychological disorder.

You do not need to feel hopeless about the scientific language emerging from brain studies. For example, you could feel discouraged by research that shows children with ADHD have brains of a smaller volume when compared with children without this diagnosis (Giedd et al. 2001). There are many scientific reasons for questioning the integrity of these findings. One critical review of neuroimaging research found that these studies examined only children treated with psychostimulants (Leo and Cohen 2003). The authors suggest that brain differences result from the medication used to treat ADHD and not ADHD itself. But at base it doesn't matter. Even if these findings were bulletproof, it would still be merely an interpretation to say that smaller volume means a deficit. Science cannot tell us that. Smaller volume could mean many things—it could mean more efficient func-tioning. Science can translate either too little or too much into pathology, as the very name of ADHD shows. Too little can be a deficit, but too much of anything can be "hyper" or a surplus.

Science and medicine are biased toward calling any difference a disorder. So, while your doctor, psychiatrist, or psychologist may have very complicated medical explanations for your child's disorder, you need not be fully convinced that he has actual brain pathology. You may read new studies in the newspaper or popular magazines that seemingly prove that there are brain differences and pathology related to ADHD. There may, in fact, be significant brain differences, but these do not have to indicate brain disorders.

There are also many scientific reasons for questioning these studies. When you read about them, you might consider that there are often many studies that show conflicting and contrary results to what you see in the media, but only the dramatic studies get media attention. You might also want to consider that in any study, conclusions are based on statistical differences, and that for any finding, there are some children with ADHD who don't show these differences and some children without ADHD who do. The conclusions presented in these studies generally represent what is found on average.

Additionally, these findings are all correlational, not experimental. This means that these studies do not involve rigorous controls that allow us to rule out many plausible alternative explanations for the relationship between ADHD and brain imaging. It only shows that individuals with ADHD demonstrate differences, not that ADHD causes these differences. Some have even argued that the brain differences might be caused by the medications used to treat ADHD. Or, for all we know, the loss of self-esteem caused by receiving the diagnosis may lead to differences in brain structure.

In short, do not be discouraged by the emerging, seemingly incontrovertible scientific reports that ADHD is a medical disorder and that there is proof that it is associated with brain pathology. First, the science is questionable. Even if there are brain differences, they don't necessarily constitute a disorder. Media reports always gloss over the fact that there are contradictory findings, that statistical differences are much weaker than people imagine, and that none of these studies can say anything about what causes the differences.

It's important for you and your child to be able to question these emerging findings because, as we have reviewed in the introduction, the belief that the differences you see in your child are part of a medical disorder related to brain pathology and therefore unchangeable creates expectations that can make it more difficult to help yourself and your child. You can change his behavior and emotional impulsivity. But you and your child will need to believe that change is possible and expect to see improvements through the exercises described in this book.

LOSS OF SELF-ESTEEM DUE TO DIAGNOSIS

One of the reasons it is so important to understand that a difference is not a disorder is because the notion that it is a disorder may undermine your child's self-esteem. Any medical or psychological diagnosis can have this effect, but particularly ADHD (Migden 2002). A diagnosis can become a central aspect of a person's identity. With a diagnosis that has the words "deficit" and "disorder" in it, the person may begin to see themself as simply defective. As described later in this chapter, the diagnosis may convey to your child these beliefs:

- He has a disease.

- He is a victim of a disease and therefore is not in control of his behavior.

- The self is fundamentally untrustworthy because it is disordered or ill.

All of these messages are potentially communicated by the diagnosis and can lead to low self-esteem. In fact, this sense of shaken or damaged identity can, in itself, lead to behavioral problems that look remarkably like ADHD, resulting in a vicious circle. We can see how this dynamic often plays out in Mike's story below.

The Legacy of a Diagnosis

Mike was a twenty-one-year-old student at a Midwestern university. He was a psychology major but was unsure what career path he would follow. He described himself as struggling with the task of, in his own words, "growing up." He described himself as having difficulties acclimating to society because of repeated failure experiences in the academic arena. He had been a C student in grade school, high school, and college. He attributed his lack of success to poor habits and a lack of motivation. Since he was a child, he had been diagnosed many times with ADHD and had undergone repeated testing. He described his academic experience as an "eternal struggle." Mike thought that the fact that he had a disorder made it impossible for him to succeed. He believed that having a disorder meant that he was not talented and that everybody else had something he didn't. He even told his psychologist that what made him the most sick was this idea that there was something fundamentally wrong with him. He said that when he compared himself to others he believed that he was handicapped, that he couldn't even compete with or compare himself to them because his disorder meant he was worse than other people. He said his diagnosis of ADHD meant more than that he simply had problems reading books. It felt to him like it meant that he could not succeed in school or in life, really. Mike thought that the diagnosis meant that he was, on the whole, a failure.

He didn't have any self-confidence in school because the diagnosis told him he was not good enough, that he was lacking something essential. Mike told his therapist that the diagnosis pervaded all areas of his life, making him feel just plain rotten. He said that it was hard enough to have to struggle in school, but almost impossible when the diagnosis made him believe that he didn't have what it takes to do well. He told his therapist that he could not see why he should even try if the diagnosis meant he was a complete failure. All of these negative feelings made him want to avoid his schoolwork and try to stay out of school as much as possible. Yet coming from a family of exceptional academic achievement made Mike think that he had no choice but to get a college education.

Mike's reflections suggest that his avoidance of academic pursuits was in part a result of the diagnosis. Having been told that he had a deficit disorder, he avoided the arena (academic) in which he understood himself to be flawed. His lack of interest and motivation in this arena can be attributed to what he called a "survival instinct." Mike believed that because he was destined to fail, he could keep his self-esteem intact by not trying. Whereas typically this lack of interest is taken to be a symptom of the disorder, his experience suggested the possibility that this behavior may actually be a symptom of the diagnosis itself. His experience also poignantly illustrates the extent to which the label impacted his core sense of self.

Mike's reflections on his experience of receiving the label of ADHD reveal that the diagnosis itself and his beliefs about it helped hold him back. His comments illustrated that "diagnoses act like computer viruses, changing and erasing memories" (Hillman and Ventura 1992, 74). Additionally, psychologist James Hillman has warned:

> The force of diagnostic stories cannot be exaggerated. Once one has been written into a particular clinical fantasy with its expectations, its typicalities, its character traits, and the rich vocabulary it offers for recognizing oneself, one then begins to recapitulate one's life into the shape of the story.... A diagnosis is indeed a gnosis: a mode of self-knowledge that creates a cosmos in its image. (Hillman 1983, 15)

The diagnosis contributed to Mike's sense of worthlessness, which exacerbated and even helped create the very symptoms that seemed to confirm the label's validity.

Mike's comments illustrate that not only can low self-esteem result from a diagnosis of ADHD, but also the lack of motivation in school was, in part, a result of the diagnosis. Because he believed himself to be handicapped in the school setting, the diagnosis led to a "why try" attitude. So, while this illustrates the impact of the diagnosis, it also points to one area that this book will help address—changing your child's thoughts about herself to gain improvements in her symptoms.

Mike felt flawed and hopeless in part because he had been given a medical diagnosis that told him he had a disorder. This idea that his differences constituted a flaw or disorder also came from his interactions with teachers. The two main culprits that lead to the emphasis on understanding the traits of ADHD as a disorder are the mental-health system and the educational system.

THE MENTAL-HEALTH SYSTEM

While your psychologist, psychiatrist, or pediatrician may seem like an authority that you cannot challenge, there is a fundamental mistake many mental-health-care providers make. A current trend in the mental-health system is toward understanding psychological issues in terms of a medical model (Furman 2002). The medical model means understanding behavioral symptoms as organic diseases that should be treated with medical interventions. In the case of ADHD, the medical model presents ADHD as a brain dysfunction to be treated with medication that changes an individual by changing the biology of the brain.

Some have argued that the move in psychology toward the medical model is influenced by the attempt to gain credibility and funding from insurance companies. Adopting a medical model serves the interest of treatment providers receiving reimbursement for their services.

The Problems with the Medical Model

While medicalizing psychological symptoms may serve insurance companies and practitioners, it may not always be in the best interest of clients. By calling psychological disturbances a disease, mental-health practitioners fail to consider the ways in which symptoms are meaningful in the context of clients' lives (Leitner, Faidley, and Celentana 2000). As a simple example, a child who has experienced family stressors and peer rejection and failure at school may disrupt the classroom as an expression of anxiety and anger at an environment that they perceive as punishing. In this way, one of the symptoms of ADHD can be seen as meaningful from the child's perspective rather than as a medical disease.

Subjective Assessment

One significant problem with the medical model is that it misrepresents the process of diagnosis, which is necessarily subjective. One thing we know is that since the symptoms themselves are behaviors rather than biological symptoms, such as fever, that the assessment of the disturbance is essentially a social judgment. In short, if a teacher is telling you that your child's behavior is unmanageable, there is no thermometer that can confirm the teacher's judgment in an objective sense. As a social judgment, the assessment is biased according to the person making the judgment and also the system or social setting in which the behavior occurs. For example, not only may there be a bias in the person making the judgment, but there may be a real problem in the social setting that your child is responding to. For example, recall Jack's story, where the young boy was responding to a setting that was harshly judgmental and lacking in caring or support for his predicament. His behavior became out of control in response to a punitive care provider. So when psychologists provide a label that carries the weight of a medical diagnosis, they are in some ways making a mistake in transferring medical notions, which are more objective, to the psychological and behavioral realm, which can only be measured in subjective and biased ways by individuals in particular settings.

Undermining Treatment Possibilities

The medical model for understanding ADHD has a lot of problems in terms of treatment. The diagnosis itself puts up a barrier to changing behavior by seeming to convey an irrefutable medical diagnosis rooted in brain pathology. Unlike more stable medical diagnoses, the realms of behavior and emotion are considerably affected by how much you and your child believe and expect that he is capable of changing his behavior. The more you believe this, the more success you will have in effecting the changes you and your child want to make.

The misperception of ADHD as a medical disorder sets up a profound barrier to treating the symptoms and helping your child heal. Because behavior and emotions are shaped so powerfully by expectations and because the label of ADHD sets up strong expectations, the label itself can be damaging. For example, if a person has Alzheimer's disease and the disorder is a progressive one, the biological course of that disorder will not be affected very much by what the doctor tells the person about the disorder. However, with psychological and behavioral symptoms, the expectations that are conveyed to you by health professionals are powerful in impacting the course of the symptoms and behavior. As a simple example, if you tell a child he has a deficit, you can expect that he will come to understand himself as flawed and that he'll act out in ways that reflect diminished self-esteem.

The label affects other people too. If a teacher is given the information that your child has ADHD, that teacher will likely act in ways toward your child that convey the expectation that your child will be difficult to manage. An enormous body of information has shown us that teachers' expectations for students are very powerful in determining the subsequent performance of those students. In one of the most well-known studies, teachers were told that a certain group of students was very gifted and another group of students was average. These expectations given to the teachers did not actually reflect the abilities of the students at all. The researchers found that the students who were expected to do very well had made substantial improvements by the end of the year, whereas those for whom the teachers had lower expectations did not make substantial improvements (see Rosenthal 1987 for a review of studies). These studies demonstrate that teachers' expectations for students create a self-fulfilling prophesy. Children have a tendency to perform in ways consistent with teachers' expectations for them. Because research has shown that diagnoses of ADHD are increasingly suggested by teachers (Sax and Kautz 2003), their expectations are increasingly influencing your child's access to or admission into the mental-health system.

Another reason that the medical model does not transfer well to behavioral problems is that the diagnosis can interfere with the most potent treatments. In a medical setting, if the cure for a fever is aspirin, the aspirin will work no matter what the doctor tells you about the nature of your disorder. However, in psychological settings, the very work of therapy and healing your child is often obstructed by the diagnosis. For example, all cognitive therapies for psychological disorders involve changing the way clients think about themselves. If a child feels that it is hopeless for him to even try in school, a cognitive therapy will help your child to challenge these thoughts of hopelessness. The diagnosis of ADHD tends to undermine the power of these therapeutic interventions. The diagnosis seems to say to the child, "You have a disorder that makes you inalterably less than other students." This communication has negative effects on your child's thoughts about himself and his abilities and can conflict with otherwise powerful cognitive therapies.

The diagnosis also fails your child because it seems to convey that ADHD is immune to change without medical interventions.

This is not a fair way of representing a psychological and behavioral difference, because your child's symptoms will vary according to setting and interaction with specific individuals. You have likely noticed this yourself. Around certain people or in specific settings your child may act like an angel and in other settings the telltale behavioral symptoms emerge with intensity. This means that your child's differences are responsive to individuals and environments. In short, your child is reacting and responding to what is going on.

So, unlike a medical disorder, the symptoms vary depending on the environment. The course of the symptoms can be dramatically affected by changing environments and providing your child guidance on how to respond to situations that provoke negative behavioral symptoms. Also, the fact that these constellations of behaviors are considered a medical disorder conveys the expectation to parents, children, and teachers that behavior should be unchanging and constant. This expectation sets up the child and his environment to create behaviors that generalize across many settings. In many ways, the diagnosis creates an expectation that manifests in the very symptoms it sets out to describe.

THE EDUCATIONAL SYSTEM

A defining feature of the public educational system is that its failings reflect the lack of value our culture places on those who educate our children. Current educational systems are plagued by lack of resources that result in overcrowded classes, overburdened teachers, and inadequate support from school psychologists or social workers (Furman 2002). With these challenges, the medical model of ADHD provides the quickest fix. Providing medication to control children's behavior is easier and cheaper than developing schools that can respond to the individual needs of students.

As you'll recall, when my brother was given his diagnosis, my mother found that he could go certain years without any medications, depending on the teacher. It must have been that the diagnosis of ADHD did not carry as much baggage as it does today, and teachers were free to respond to my brother as a unique individual rather than as a troubled child. It may also have been that many teachers did not even know what the diagnosis meant, or they were not aware that he had been given this diagnosis. Today, these diagnoses follow the child from year to year, and of course every teacher knows precisely what to expect from a child given this diagnosis.

Because of this recent trend, your child is most likely walking into the classroom, even in a new year with a new teacher, with a heavy load of expectations that are not in his favor. It's not surprising that his symptoms seem so consistent from year to year, from teacher to teacher, if you consider that he's walking into the same set of expectations.

While the mental-health field has determined that your child has a deficit disorder, research has shown that children diagnosed with ADHD, on average, do not have lower IQ scores than other children (Psychological Corporation 1997). The only significant deficits are in working memory, which means that they cannot hold numbers or other information in their memory as long as other children. You can probably see that a deficit in working memory doesn't mean your child cannot succeed in the classroom. Your child's teachers may have misunderstood the diagnosis of ADHD and taken it to mean that your child is less intelligent than other students or that she is less capable of scholastic achievement than other children. Research has shown that 50 to 75 percent of a child's academic success is dependent on nonintellectual factors such as persistence, psychological health, and curiosity (Groth-Marnat 2003). This means that your child has a great deal of potential for succeeding in school, though teachers tend to view ADHD as a black mark. This book will show you that one of the gifts of ADHD is your child's enormous curiosity and energy. In addition, throughout this book you will be provided with exercises for increasing your child's persistence and personal adjustment. All of these will help your child succeed in school.

Handling Difference

The education system is not set up to handle differences among children. Even traditionally gifted children are failed by the current educational system. As it stands, the current school system focuses almost exclusively on developing one or two types of intelligence—abstract reasoning in verbal and mathematical realms and the acquisition of abstract facts and knowledge. Recent advances in psychology and education reveal that there are many different types of intelligence and that each child has a unique profile of strengths and weaknesses. Many children are failed by the exclusive and excessive focus on the development of abstract reasoning and learning through book knowledge. ADHD children are particularly failed by this system because they do not learn well by abstraction or through book knowledge.

Children with ADHD are immensely curious and interested but learn best through engaging their senses and through immersion in the organic world. If every day were a field trip, these kids would be considered geniuses. They learn by doing, by being active, by being engaged with the objects of their curiosity. The school system may pay some lip service to developing an individualized learning plan but probably won't in any significant way accommodate the true gifts and differences of your child. And, rather than recognizing the lack of flexibility of the educational system to accommodate these differences, the system and its representatives (the teachers) blame the child for not having a mind that fits its curriculum.

As with the mental-health system, this tendency to point the finger at your child rather than recognizing its own failings further exacerbates your child's problems. Rather than conveying a message that says, "You are different, and our system is not set up to meet your needs," your child gets the message, "Because you don't fit our system, you must have a disorder." The educational system and teachers are not bad people; they're not trying to hurt your child. But it is a system with profoundly limited resources and one that does not acknowledge how it fails children with significant differences.

I review these failings not to make you feel hopeless but rather to empower you in becoming an advocate for your child. In my experience, teachers and mental-health-care professionals are very caring people who want to help your child, but they are part of institutions and world views that don't work well for kids with differences. As a parent, you have enormous power to engage the individuals who work closely with your child and help to change their vision and expectations. Working on a one-to-one basis, you're more likely to have success, because these individuals want the best for you and your child. You will learn more about advocating for your child later in the book.

THE MEDICATION DEBATE

Both the educational systems and the mental-health-care systems rely on the use of medication to suppress the symptoms of ADHD. Ritalin, the most popular of these medications, is the brand name for methyl-phenidate and belongs to a classification of mood-altering drugs that stimulate brain functioning (psychostimulants). While the prescription for medication is so commonplace that most parents and teachers have stopped questioning its use, there is a great debate about using medica-tion to treat ADHD.

The theory that ADHD is a brain disease lends itself directly to the use of medication to treat it. It makes sense that if ADHD is caused by brain pathology, a drug that alters brain functioning would be the cure. Alternatively, the theory that ADHD is not a brain disease calls into question the use of medications for treating children given this diagnosis. Below we'll examine both sides of the argument on the use of medications.

Medication as the Answer

The main argument for the use of medications like Ritalin to treat ADHD is that these medications work. Simply put, they decrease the symptoms of ADHD. Children who are on Ritalin can sit still longer, can focus more, and display fewer problematic behaviors. The most recent large-scale study comparing medication to behavioral interventions found that children showed more improve-ments in ADHD symptoms if they were receiving medication than if they were only receiving behavioral treatments (MTA Cooperative Group 1999).

In this way, medication may allow your child to manage his behavior and therefore to hit appropriate developmental milestones on time. Medication has the benefit of demonstrating immediate, positive effects to the child, parents, and teachers. Parents and teachers benefit from being relieved of the constant stress of managing a child who, without medication, seems incapable of managing himself.

Why Medications May Not Be the Answer

There are many problems with using medications to treat ADHD. The first and foremost of these problems is that there is no science that tells us the long-term effects of these drugs on children. There is reason to believe that there are significant short-term and long-term negative effects of being treated with ADHD medications. Short-term negative effects include insomnia, stomach problems, irritability, headaches, and heart palpitations, among others. Long-term effects are unknown, but some have raised concerns about these drugs stunting physical, mental, and emotional development. Another concern for longer-term side effects is the potential for addiction to these drugs.

Methylphenidate, the most common medication, has been classified by the Drug Enforcement Agency of the Justice Department as a Schedule II drug, meaning that it has a high potential for abuse. Other drugs so classified include cocaine, morphine, and amphetamines—all recognizable drugs of abuse (Furman 2002). Not only is methylphenidate addictive, but it has been argued that it serves as a "gateway" drug, leading individuals to become addicted to other more serious drugs later in life (Stein 1999).

In addition to potential side effects, one criticism of using medications is that, while research has shown that these drugs work to control behavior, there is no evidence that they actually improve academic outcomes. In short, children may be more well behaved, but they don't necessarily get better grades in school (Furman 2002). So these medications allow teachers and parents to tolerate their children more easily, but there is no benefit to the child in terms of increased achievement. Even the behavioral benefits that are observed only last as long as the child is on medication. These medications do not cure the disorder—they simply suppress the symptoms while the child is on them.

Another criticism of the use of the medications is that the effects of stimulants such as methylphenidate are not specific to children diagnosed with ADHD. It has been argued that putting a child on ADHD medications is not much different than putting a child on speed to help him focus and concentrate (Stein 1999). It has also been argued that Ritalin, like any stimulant, improves mood and self-esteem (Breggin 1991). It may be that these drugs also work not by fixing brain pathology but by making children "high" so they are more motivated and feel better about themselves, and their behavior improves.

Another criticism of the use of medications is that often ADHD behaviors are caused by specific issues that the child needs to address and cope with. Common issues include losses in the family, high levels of stress in the family, and mental and physical health problems in parents or siblings, among many others. Children are very sensitive and their behavior can easily be disturbed by anxiety and loss. By suppressing the symptoms with medications, the underlying issues for the child may never get addressed and can show up in more disruptive forms later in life.

To Medicate or Not to Medicate

As a parent you will have to make your own decision, in collaboration with your child's psychiatrist, regarding medication. The bias of this book is that ADHD is a gift that is misunderstood in this culture, and that eliminating this gift by medication does not make sense. As a parent, you should be aware of the costs and benefits of medicating your child.

I've tried to outline these costs and benefits so you can make an informed choice. When looking to others for advice about whether to medicate, you shouldn't expect your child's teachers or psychiatrist to encourage you in taking your child off medication. As we've seen, both teachers and mental-health professionals have an interest in promoting medication, either for the increased manageability of your child or to adhere to a medicalized model of mental health. If your child is currently on medication and you are interested in taking your child off the drugs, an important resource is Peter Breggin's book with coauthor David Cohen called *Your Drug May Be Your Problem: How and Why to Stop Taking Psychiatric Medications,* published in 1999 by Perseus Books.

SUPPORTING YOUR CHILD

One thing researchers have determined about treating people with behavioral and emotional disorders is that the relationship to the client is one of the most powerful factors in helping that person change. So, in order for you to help your child, you must have a supportive relationship with him. Many times, the very behaviors that are problematic cause frustration in parents, making them antagonistic toward their child. This reaction is very understandable because children with ADHD do require an enormous amount of energy and atention and their behavior can test a parent's limits in many ways. Also, because of the pressures from school systems and health-care professionals, parents may find themselves becoming apologists for their children. Parents may feel compelled to apologize for their child's behavior, which amounts to an admission that the child is in the wrong. So, rather than defending your child or pointing out how what he is doing can be understood as a positive trait, parents concede too much authority to teachers by agreeing with their criticisms.

The more frustrated you become with your child, the more your child will feel hurt and will act out in ways that cause problems for others. The more you can see your child's difference as a gift rather than a disorder, the stronger your relationship will be and the more helpful you can be. The diagnosis itself can make the relationship difficult because your child may hear the diagnosis as invalidating. If your child believes that you buy into the view that he is defective, he may resent your lack of confidence in him. In order for you to use the tools in this book most effectively, you need to find ways to make your child feel that you are on his side and that you think very highly of him. Your relationship with your child will be a powerful agent for transformation.

Accept Who They Are, but Set Limits

The best way to forge a strong and supportive relationship with your child is to achieve a balance between giving your child the strong validation that he needs while at the same time communicating the need for changes to be made. Although this seems contradictory, it will make sense to your child. Because your child needs to feel safe, strong, and confident to engage the world, he will need lots of acceptance and validation just for being who he is. This book will help with that, because it will guide you in reframing the labels that have been put on your child as positive qualities, affirmation that your child deeply needs to hear.

In addition, because your child is still early in his development, he recognizes that he needs the support, direction, and guidance of his parents. Your child may not communicate this to you directly, but it is a fundamental need of any child to receive direction and feedback. At heart, children recognize that they would be in trouble if they ruled the world. In fact, many behavioral disturbances are efforts to engage parents in setting limits. Children get very anxious if they have too much power and need reassurance that their parents are strong and will set limits when needed. Your child may communicate exactly the opposite to you and tell you to leave him alone, but inside he is crying out for direction and guidance. So, your child will also respond positively to your efforts to change her behavior if you set strong boundaries while communicating a feeling of love for who he is.

The organization of this book will help you achieve this delicate balance. Because the foundation of the book is reframing ADHD as a gift, you can use the awareness and cognitive exercises to communicate to your child that you love and accept the very traits that others are calling problems. The behavioral strategies will also help you to communicate to your child that you care so much, you will play an active role in guiding his behavior and that you will be willing to set limits when needed. For instance, exercises will guide you to help yourself and your child understand that the symptom of hyperactivity can also be understood as an abundance of energy. In this way, you are validating the child. In addition to this, you will also be guided to help your child become aware of ways in which expression of this energy becomes distracting to others in school settings, and you'll learn techniques for shaping your child's behavior in ways that reduce the frequency of these distracting behaviors.

Believe Change Is Possible

Another reason for you to counteract the effects of the label ADHD is because in order for your child to make changes, he needs to believe that change is possible. Because it seems to carry the weight of a medical diagnosis and is often misunderstood as a brain disorder, the label of ADHD conveys the subtle message to your child that this is a disorder that is intrinsic to who he is, and that he therefore cannot change the resulting behavior and symptoms. The traits of ADHD may have some of their roots in the brain, but to label those traits and the brain differences as a disorder or disease is a mistake. Somehow the impression that ADHD is like a medical disease makes it feel to you and your child that it is not possible to make internal changes that will turn things around. However, ADHD is not like a medical disease, in that it is not something a child "has" but a description of a set of behaviors the child does. For this reason, it is important that if your child has been given this diagnosis that you, as a parent, provide balance by reframing the disorder as a difference and assuring your child that they can change their behavior.

Increase Motivation to Change

Another way in which reframing the diagnosis of ADHD will help you and your child is by increasing your motivation and your child's motivation for change. The field of psychology is just recently being changed by the idea that clients have different levels of readiness to change. Many interventions are offered to clients with the assumption that they are highly motivated to make changes in their lives, but this is often untrue. Many clients are resistant to change for many reasons. With ADHD, you and your child may not be motivated to undertake the work required to follow through on these exercises because you feel hopeless. Why exert so much effort to change if your doctor has told you that it is a brain disorder and that the only treatment is medications that change the brain chemistry? Isn't it easier to take pills than to work hard to change behaviors and emotions? This is how the medical model decreases your motivation.

In order for you to feel motivated to change and to increase your child's motivation for change, you have to believe that your hard work will pay off. By reframing the disorder as gift, understanding the significant resources your child has, and conveying this to your child, you can increase motivation for making changes. Many of the strategies and exercises you'll learn in this book will require some commitment of time and energy from you and your child. In order to follow through you will need motivation and an expectation that this investment will yield benefits for both you and your child. By understanding the nature of your child's gifts you will likely have more hope for your child and therefore feel more engaged and willing to do the hard work of helping him change.

You can also increase your motivation to follow through on the exercises by viewing them as a chance for you to reconnect with your child. You may want to reframe your interactions with your child as guided by this book as "play time." You can set up a specific, special time to do them, and you and your child can engage in them together in the spirit of fun. As a parent, you have the power to reframe the exercises in this book as an opportunity to spend time together and to work toward a common goal. The exercises are designed to be appealing to children and to use images that evoke fun and play. For example, in chapter 9, when we discuss managing emotions, an exercise is provided for surfing the waves of emotion. Thus the exercises try to evoke fun activities and show your child how managing and connecting with his own experience can also be fun and playful. If you take such an attitude and play with your child in these exercises, you can serve as a powerful model for your child.

Put Your Child In Control of ADHD

The diagnosis may seem to carry the subtle message that your child is a victim of a disorder and that he is therefore less capable of making choices. Sometimes parents or children think that because ADHD is a disorder they passively suffer from, that the kids are not in control of and therefore not responsible for their behavior. To the extent that the label itself conveys the idea that children are not responsible for their behavior ("My ADHD made me do it"), they are more likely to act out in impulsive and irresponsible ways.

The diagnosis of ADHD also serves as a barrier to healing because it conveys to you and your child that your child's experiences are untrustworthy—meaning that his experiences are not reliable for guiding actions. The pathway to healing from ADHD includes a gain in self-esteem so he can trust himself to make important life choices and commitments. For example, children with ADHD often have an uncanny ability to read others. Often because they express these insights in irreverent ways, they are punished for the expression of this gift. They then come to doubt their own perceptions. The inability to trust their own perceptions leads to conflict and confusion in interpersonal relationships and lowered self-esteem. These two consequences lead to disturbance in relating to others. In this way, the inability to trust their own experience—again, in part a consequence of the diagnosis—leads to some of the very symptoms the diagnosis points to.

The fundamental issue for changing behavior is for you to recognize that your child *can* control some of the behaviors that are problematic. This book will guide you in becoming aware of how your child can reclaim control and how you can guide him toward seeing his own power over his thoughts, feelings, and behaviors.

Summary

As a parent of a child with ADHD, your job is really cut out for you. You probably struggle with your own feelings of hopelessness about changing your child. You struggle with your child's motivation to change. Mental-health-care and educational systems may seem overly eager to change your child in ways with which you may not be fully comfortable. While navigating all of these complexly interacting pieces may seem overwhelming, the goal of reclaiming your child's gifts from the cloud of the medicalized diagnosis of ADHD is worth it. You have the power to connect to your own delight in your child's differences and to share your vision of your child as gifted with your child, your child's teachers, and other significant individuals in your child's life.

Most importantly, through reclaiming the power of a supportive and validating relationship with your child, you reconnect with your child and have the relationship with him that you truly want. The healing of this relationship will be the most powerful agent of healing your child.

CHAPTER 2

How You Can Transform Your Child

COGNITIVE BEHAVIORAL THERAPY

One of the leading methods of therapy today for treating a wide range of psychological and behavioral problems is called *cognitive behavioral therapy* or CBT. This type of therapy focuses on current thoughts and behaviors that create symptoms. One way to break this vicious cycle is to intervene at the level of thoughts and attitudes.

A cognitive behavioral therapist will actively work to challenge irrational and unproductive thoughts and attitudes, helping the client change them to attitudes and beliefs that will lead to more productive behaviors. One of the central assumptions of the cognitive behavioral approach offered in this book is that thoughts cause feelings and behaviors. Therefore, changing thoughts or challenging your child's self-defeating thoughts can help her manage feelings and behaviors. Additionally, changing behaviors can impact thoughts and feelings.

Sometimes therapists will ask clients to directly change behaviors and observe changes in thoughts and feelings that follow.

Throughout this book, you will be offered many different exercises and strategies for helping your child identify and challenge thoughts that lead to disrupted behaviors. The cognitive behavioral approach also relies on breaking big behavior changes down to very small and manageable tasks. This helps increase motivation by not asking for sweeping, permanent changes all at once. Also, by identifying and meeting small challenges, your child will have success earlier and more consistently, which will further increase motivation to keep making changes.

YOUR POWER TO ASSIST IN CHANGE

As a parent, you have the power to identify and shape your child's attitudes and behaviors. This book will provide you with a rich resource and specific strategies, techniques, and playful exercises for helping your child adopt the most positive thoughts and attitudes. Many of the exercises can be framed as games and can go a long way toward breaking the vicious cycle that can make your child's differences seem like a deficit. When you cast the exercises as pretend games, your child cannot fail. It's all pretend, it's a game, so these exercises are less likely to backfire and make your child more discouraged if she doesn't fully follow through. Similarly, if the exercises are cast as experiments where the point is to find out how this new attitude or thought impacts the child's experience, there is no way for her to fail.

The way to get your child to sign on to a healing program is to captivate her interest in the process by making it a game. One of the challenges of treating symptoms of ADHD is engaging and motivating kids who have trouble paying attention or following through on almost anything. After all, if she could follow the treatment program, she wouldn't be exhibiting the symptoms that are so problematic. For this reason, treatment programs or self-help programs that rely on discipline from the child are likely to fail. This program of change has been designed to channel the existing high level of energy, curiosity, and areas of interest of your child to help her *want* to engage.

Strengthen the Bond with Your Child

While this program will not demand of your child skills that she doesn't have, it will demand a commitment from you as the parent. However, you will find that the exercises are meant to be like a form of play and will therefore serve to strengthen your bond and relationship with your child. This is not an extra chore—it is part of your existing commitment to spend more time with your child and to enrich your relationships.

Sometimes parents are hesitant to implement suggestions from self-help books or mental-health practitioners because they feel it pits them against their own child, or adds to the burden of parenting rather than adding to the joy. The exercises in this book not only may help your child with the specific problem of ADHD, but may also address your more general problem of how to spend quality time with your child. These exercises will help to increase your intimacy with your child, and because they are validating for your child and cast as play, will not require you to pit your will against your child in getting her to conform to a demanding program for reform.

Reframe

Revisioning ADHD as a gift will help to increase your child's motivation by offering praise for the very symptoms that others have found so problematic. The revisioning of the diagnosis is an example of a central cognitive behavioral technique for treating any disorder: reframing. In reframing, you change your *cognitive interpretation* of (the way you think about) some trait about yourself or some event in the real world that has upset you. For example, if you find out that someone you are close to did not tell you something major that was happening in his or her life, you might get upset and think he or she is trying to keep secrets from you. A reframing of this might be that this person did not tell you what was going on to protect you by not getting you upset. As you can probably imagine, the emotions and behavior that will follow these different interpretations will be quite different.

The strategy of finding alternative interpretations for events and characteristics of the self is a central method of change in cognitive behavioral therapy, the approach for change used in this book. Helping your child to reframe the diagnosis of ADHD as a gift that makes her different from others in potentially positive ways is central in helping your child. Not only will the reframing help as a strategy in and of itself, it will provide the motivation for engaging in the program of change offered in this book.

Increase Motivation to Change

One reason many treatments fail is that the program of change or the therapist operate under the assumption that the person who needs help is motivated and ready to change. This assumption is often wrong. Therapists often blame their clients for not wanting to change, or individuals will heap more blame on themselves for their failure to follow through on rigorous programs for reforming the self. Understanding ADHD as a gift will get around this problem for two main reasons: first, you are increasing motivation by elevating your child's self-esteem, and second, you are validating your child by conveying the message that who she is is fundamentally okay. You are not trying to eliminate a disorder, you are trying to shape your child so that she can use these differences in ways that help her meet her goals.

The most important thing is to cast this program so that it isn't about changing who your child is, but rather helps her achieve the goals that she really wants to achieve. In this way, you are not working against your child but are offering your time and energy to help her get what she wants. Children with ADHD want to be liked by their peers and teachers, and they want to excel and be respected for their abilities, but they have a hard time doing these things when their differences have not yet begun to be appreciated.

EXERCISES FOR SPECIFIC CHALLENGES

The rest of the chapter will be devoted to learning exercises to address specific symptoms of ADHD. You may want to read through all the exercises first and then use the ones that you and your child will feel most comfortable with. There are many exercises throughout the book, and it's important that you find a handful of exercises that you and your child really enjoy and that don't feel like chores. If you and your child can engage in some of the exercises regularly, you can expect to see your child (and your relationship with her) transform. The exercises are designed to tap into your child's existing interests and strengths, so they should be presented to your child as fun games rather than as a reform strategy. You can find creative ways to integrate these games into your lives. For example, some of the pretend games can be played while driving in the car or sitting in a waiting room. If your child doesn't like some of the games, you don't have to push it. Try some of the others to find some that she really likes and repeat those exercises.

The Challenge of Persistence

One of the most well-documented differences between individuals diagnosed with ADHD and other children is that they do not persist as long as other children do in academic tasks. Studies have found that ADHD children who are asked to solve cognitive puzzles will have less success and will quit working more often than others (Hoza et al. 2001). In addition, observers rated ADHD children as putting forth less effort and being less cooperative than those in a control group. The following exercise will help address this characterization of children diagnosed with ADHD. A typical strategy in cognitive behavioral therapy is for the therapist to ask the client to evaluate the costs and benefits of a particular thought, belief, or attitude. The exercise that follows invites your child to imagine the consequences over time of a belief that she does not need to work hard.

EXERCISE: WHY TRY?

When your child makes comments to the effect of "why try?" you can offer many different helpful responses. Try the following exercise with your child next time she expresses this sort of dysfunctional attitude in response to challenges. This exercise will demonstrate to your child how this thought is very powerful and can lead to self-defeating behaviors.

- ■   Ask your child to imagine her favorite superhero or cartoon, movie, or book character and ask her how that character's life would be different if they adopted a "why try?" attitude.

- ■   The more concrete you can make this exercise the better. For example, after watching a specific episode of a cartoon or after leaving a specific movie, ask your child what would have happened differently in that story if the character had said "why try?"

In this way, your child can begin to understand the power of thoughts in impacting the outcome of life and affecting her own success or failure. By starting out with characters, your child can explore this powerful principle in a displaced manner that is less threatening than thinking directly about her own attitudes.

Recognizing Your Child's Interests

Children with ADHD think organically and imaginally. They struggle with abstract reasoning that is removed from everyday life and their interests. They are often ardently curious and have passions in specific areas of specialization. They can be highly motivated if you engage these areas of intense interest.

The tricky part about cognitive interventions is that, on the one hand, you want to change your child's thoughts and behavior, and on the other hand, children with ADHD are in deep need of validation and acceptance of who they are exactly as they are. For this reason, one strategy for teaching some of the basic principles is to start out with fictional characters that your child already has a passionate interest in. As in the preceding exercise, because you are talking about a character, your child will be less likely to become defensive and antagonistic toward you. She will not be as likely to feel invalidated. As a rule, you will want to work with your child's passionate interests even if those interests seem like distractions or not academic enough.

Children with ADHD often channel much of their energy and enthusiasm toward what seems like a waste of time. They may get very excited about sports figures, sports teams, animals, dinosaurs, or subject areas that don't seem likely to lead to academic success. One of the major themes of this book will be that these areas of intense interest are tremendous resources for you to tap into. For example, if your child loves figure skating and identifies Sarah Hughes as a hero, you can use that energy and channel it toward making concrete behavioral change. At times when your child gets discouraged about school and says things like she's not good enough because of the ADHD, you can ask her to think through what would Sarah Hughes's life be like if she had said "Why try?

In one example, a seven-year-old boy was obsessed with knights. He talked about knights with shining armor, he often drew pictures of knights, and he loved to read stories and see movies that involved knights. In this case, both the teachers and the parents were worried about this preoccupation and wondered if, in itself, it might represent a separate disorder—some form of childhood obsessive-compulsive disorder. However, all children, and particularly children with ADHD, are quite imaginative and intense in their interests. Rather than communicating your anxiety about these sorts of preoccupations to your child, you can channel the energy around these interests into productive work or to help increase motivation.

EXERCISE: THE KNIGHTS

If your child was interested in knights, you could invite him to play a game where you explore the outcomes of two different knights, Sir Try-a-Lot and Sir Why-Try. For older children, you may want to choose sports heros rather than fictional characters. As an example, you might use Lance Armstrong, the cyclist who has repeatedly won the Tour de France after recovering from cancer.

1. Set up a typical scenario or ask your child to provide the details of the challenges to be overcome, perhaps including a dragon guarding a treasure and a damsel in distress. Embellish your

story to make as many parallels as possible to your child's own language and attitudes around the diagnosis of ADHD. For example, you might say that both knights were told by the King that because they had a handicap, they could not be a part of the round table, and so each knight set out to find adventures on their own. As you invite your child to elaborate on the fortunes of these two different knights—one that keeps trying harder and harder in the face of challenges and one that says "why try?"—draw out the major themes for your child. These themes will include the power of a positive attitude to achieve goals and how our thoughts create our behavior.

2. As a parent, let your child's imagination run wild as he explores the different fates of the two knights (or other characters that are of interest). Then you can gently bring him back to applying these principles to his own life. You might gently remind him, for example, how this would apply to his struggles in social studies class, where your child feels the teacher is always "dissing" him. Be careful to extend this period of application only as long as your child will tolerate. When he shows signs of distress, boredom, or the typical symptoms of hyperactivity, let him guide the conversation back to the imaginal arena or whatever is of more interest to him. When you push too hard on the application or the moral of the story he will come to resent these games and will become bored by them. In trying to help your child heal from his difficulty paying attention, you must validate and cater to the very symptoms you are trying to help him overcome. So don't resist his lack of attention. You can maintain his attention by returning as often as necessary to his area of intense interest, be it knights, sports, or something else, and embedding the exercises within these contexts.

3. As you engage your child in these exercises, encourage him to identify thoughts leading to emotions that might make a character say "why try?" Help him see the connection between these thoughts, emotions, and the behaviors they encourage. Then challenge him to generate ideas or thoughts that would help the characters to overcome their challenges

or to achieve their goals. Cast this again as an imaginal or exploratory game. If a knight was banished from the round table for having a handicap that made everyone think he wasn't as capable as the other knights, what might he say to himself to become a hero? Ask your child to write down examples of things this character could say to himself that would be helpful. Help your child if he is struggling. For example, you might suggest that the knight says, "Well, I can do whatever those other knights can do, I just have to try harder." In this way, the diagnosis of ADHD can be seen as a spur to more effort rather than an incentive to give up in frustration. Again, it is important to be sensitive to your child's attention span in playing this game. You may want to play it over and over again in different times and settings rather than drawing it out over long periods of time.

EXERCISE: BE YOUR HERO

1. You can increase the effectiveness of the preceding technique by challenging your child to a pretend game. For example, you might say, "This next week, when you feel that Ms. Wyatt is dissing you, why don't you try to be like the knight who was banished from the round table and try even harder in the course material?" Tell your child it's a game to play just for one week, or frame it as an experiment to see what effect it has on the teacher. In this way, you can provoke your child's interest. Be careful each day to remind your child about your pretend game and then to follow up after school on what happened in the game.

2. Start out by focusing on one problem area. For example, use one teacher or class that is particularly distressing for your child. This way, she is likely to be able to follow through and meet with some early successes. If you start by suggesting that she be the knight in all her classes, your child may not be able to follow through on the amount of exertion required to make such a sweeping change and could give up in frustration. By starting out in one class for one week, your child may be highly

motivated to follow through and won't feel overwhelmed by the prospect of dramatically changing her behavior overnight.

Engage Your Child's Senses

Your child learns through being engaged with the world, by touching, tasting, feeling, and being actively immersed in what she is trying to learn. This is important to keep in mind when deciding how you will engage her in this healing program. Your child will have a very low tolerance for lectures or moralizing, as she has difficulty (and little interest) in wading through abstract information. This means that separating facts and figures from their real-world context is almost intolerably boring for your child.

While the previous exercises activated your child's imagination, the following exercise illustrates how you can use concrete sensory objects to impress on your child the principles of cognitive behavioral therapy. You will help your child see that when the attitudes that lead to low persistence are put under the microscope of rational scrutiny, they are obviously unproductive. Whereas typical CBT interventions with adults involve lengthy homework assignments and rigorous analysis of thoughts and behaviors, children with a diagnosis of ADHD will not tolerate those kinds of abstract exercises requiring concentration and patience. So, this next exercise makes the process fun.

In addition to making concrete the process of examining her thought processes, the following exercises will serve to increase your child's commitment to this program of transformation. The more clearly your child is able to see how her thought patterns are self-defeating, the more she will be willing to engage in the other exercises.

EXERCISE: THE BALANCE

1. Obtain a two-sided balance or scale where you can put objects on both sides and see which side is heavier. You will be able to use this scale for many exercises described in this book,

helping your child evaluate the costs and benefits of her thoughts, beliefs, attitudes, or behaviors. If you cannot find a scale, you can do this exercise by drawing a teeter-totter on a piece of paper, writing the costs on one side of the teeter-totter, and benefits on the other, and asking your child to identify which list would weigh that side of the teeter-totter down. For an older child, you could ask her to draw a picture of a scale with lines below each side to fill in with costs and benefits. Bring also a bunch of pennies to work with.

2. Sit down with your child and the scale or drawing of a scale or teeter-totter. Work with her to identify one of her self-defeating thoughts, like "Why should I try if I have a deficit disorder?" You might do this by asking her what she was thinking just before a recent distracted or frustrated behavior.

3. Invite your child to evaluate the costs and benefits of the belief by asking her to think of all the reasons that her belief is good for her. Designate one side of the scale as the side that weighs the benefits of this belief.

4. Identify the other side of the scale as the side that you'll use to weigh the costs of the belief or ways in which the belief is hurtful to the child. Then encourage her to come up with some of these ways. Start with how the belief is helpful, as she will likely have more energy around that, and this will allow you to keep her attention and gain momentum for the game. Place a penny on the appropriate side of the scale for each reason your child thinks of. She might say that this belief prevents her from trying and failing and getting hurt or any number of possible reasons.

5. If she's struggling for ideas and hasn't hit on this one, help her by suggesting that the belief prevents her from getting hurt. It may be helpful to make explicit this primary motivation for avoiding schoolwork.

6. After you have completed the positive side, you can then say, "Okay, let's put some pennies on the other side of the scale for all the reasons you can think of that this belief will hurt you. What can you think of?" Your child might suggest "By

saying 'why try?' to myself, I don't work very hard, and I don't do very well." She might say that the belief makes her feel hopeless. She might say that she doesn't get good grades in school because of this belief. On this side, encourage her and give as many hints and suggestions as possible for making this a very long list. The idea is to generate examples of how this thought leads to negative emotions and negative behaviors, leading her to do poorly in school. Create as many examples as you can and make them as concrete as possible. For instance, you can include not only that this belief leads her to not do as well as she could in school, but specifically that it leads her to get a particular grade in a particular class. You will want to elaborate with as many specific and concrete examples as you and your child can imagine. For every example, put a penny on the appropriate side of the scale.

7. Finally, show your child how the side that is weighing the costs is so much heavier than the side that is weighing benefits. You may want to briefly but explicitly make a connection as to how this disparity in weight might cause her to want to change the belief. Remember, she won't be able to tolerate the "moral of the story" for very long.

As a rule you will have more success with these exercises if you follow these guidelines:

- Keep the game embedded in the play aspect and avoid abstract moralizing.

- Do the exercises frequently for many different situations, as your child does not generalize very easily.

- Refer to your child's thoughts as "what you say to yourself."

Be prepared for your child to have some difficulty identifying her thoughts and attitudes, again because it is asking her to abstract from her immediate experience. Also, understand that your child has such a low tolerance for moralizing because all moralizing conveys the implicit message that she is wrong or something she is doing is wrong. This sounds to her like invalidation. Kids with ADHD are particularly sensitive and intuitive in regard to picking up the underlying messages of interpersonal interactions, which tends to give them a low threshold for being invalidated. It is like the world has turned up the volume to an unbearably high level and any implied, subtle, or well-meaning efforts to reform your child will be heard by her as stinging condemnation. Also bear in mind that the diagnosis of ADHD itself can be a profound invalidation of her way of being in the world. Any person, and certainly any sensitive child, can only take so much invalidation.

For this reason, you will have more success with your child if you engage her senses in using the exercises in this book and work to increase her own motivation to change rather than imposing it on her in a moralizing way. There are many strategies and activities you can do to make your child's desire to change come from within, rather than from a wish to please you, teachers, or mental-health-care professionals. These strategies are incorporated into the exercises in this book.

The exercises we've looked at so far will have helped your child to see how her self-defeating beliefs don't really help her. This will have helped motivate her to begin to change some of those beliefs. The following exercise provides an opportunity to explicitly introduce your child to a program for transformation using cognitive behavioral therapy. By engaging her senses, she will come to see how CBT makes sense and how it can help her.

EXERCISE: DETECTIVES, WIZARDS, AND WINNERS—OH MY!

1. Start by collecting the following items: a hat that your child can wear as a detective's hat, a magic wand (available at party or joke stores, or easily made with tape and a pencil), a stuffed heart (available in card stores or toy stores), and finally, a toy trophy. These items will help externalize inner processes for your child and help her to understand the basics of the CBT

approach used in this book. The detective hat will symbolize her ability to discover thoughts that create emotions and behaviors; the magic wand will symbolize her capacity to imagine a better outcome; the stuffed heart will symbolize her feelings; and the trophy will represent her changed behavior.

2. Invite your child to play a game called something like the "Sherlock Holmes Game" or the "Detective Game."

3. Describe to your child that, like sleuths, you're going to work together to find and uncover the beliefs that cause problems and change those beliefs to create the outcomes that she wants.

4. Briefly describe cognitive behavioral theory in a way your child will understand. Explain about thoughts leading to emotions leading to behavior. Set this up so that it is interesting for your child by engaging her about a concrete issue that she is struggling with. To make this fun for her, give her the detective's hat to wear as she tries to find the trail of thinking that has led to problematic feelings and behaviors.

5. Once your child has identified some specific thoughts that are creating problems, you can let her know that now she can pretend to be a wizard. Give your child the magic wand, which represents her ability to imagine a better outcome. Ask her to pretend to be the wizard and tell you what magic she would create if the magic wand gave her unlimited powers. This is meant to help your child expand her thinking to imagine the most positive possible alternative outcome.

6. Once your child has imagined the best possible alternative outcome, you can show her how the heart symbolizes her feelings and how the trophy symbolizes her successful resolution of the problem. Invite her to think about how she would feel if she changed her problematic thoughts and how she could achieve the desired outcome.

As an example of how to play this game, imagine that your child has come home complaining that she is doing terribly in her social studies class. You would invite her to play the detective game, shaping it to meet her interests. You could give her the magic wand

and ask her to make a wish of how she would like things to turn out. Then you could ask her what thoughts she would need to have to make that happen. You might invite her to put on the detective hat and investigate what she could say to herself that would help make her wish come true. She might identify thoughts like, "I would have to believe that I could do better if I tried harder," or "I would have to believe that even though it's hard, I can learn how to concentrate." Then you could ask her to hold the stuffed heart and identify how these thoughts would make her feel. She might realize that by believing that she could achieve her goals through hard work, she'll feel more hopeful or determined to do better. Then you can use the trophy to symbolize a concrete behavior that would help make her wish come true. You might help your child identify that if she worked on social studies for one hour each night, she would be more likely to achieve her dream.

By engaging your child's senses and imagination you will have much more luck in making these exercises interesting for your child. Success also depends on you tapping into an existing area of intense interest for your child. So for example, if your child loves Harry Potter, you can ask her to think about Harry Potter rather than just a generic wizard.

CHALLENGING SELF-BLAME

Because having a child diagnosed with ADHD affects the whole family, you, your child, and your other children will benefit if you apply some of the principles of cognitive behavioral therapy to yourself. Because of your engagement in the mental-health and school systems you may have come to feel like you made some serious mistakes as a parent or that you are somehow to blame for your child's diagnosis. Sometimes, the diagnosis of ADHD in a child can have a serious negative impact on parents as they begin to doubt not only their abilities as a parent but their own sense of self-worth. You may begin to feel that you're not good enough or that no matter how hard you try, you cannot do well as a parent. You may begin to feel inferior to other parents. You may feel ashamed when meeting with teachers and doctors about your child's behavior. These are normal reactions, but there is much to do to counter these notions and feel better. And, as you help yourself, you will also be helping your child.

If you start to feel depressed and lose interest in activities that used to be pleasurable, you can benefit from trying some of these cognitive behavioral interventions on yourself. Because your child with ADHD is so sensitive, she will be dramatically affected by your state of mind. So anything you can do to help yourself will indirectly help your child. It will also help directly, because as you help yourself, you will be more patient and loving toward your child. You will also have more energy to spend quality time with your child and build the relationship that will be the foundation for coping with and transforming the diagnosis of ADHD.

Some of the popular literature on ADHD blames parents for the child's disorder, pinning the genesis of the problem on parental abuse or neglect. Also, teachers who may want to shift the blame away from the way they manage their classroom may be too eager to place the blame on parents. But even if you've never read any of this literature or been blamed for the diagnosis by a teacher, you may have been haunted by the fear that somehow you are culpable. Mothers are particularly prone to feeling responsible and may even wonder if ADHD was the result of something they did while they were pregnant. As a mother, the potential sources of self-blame are endless.

Try to remember that the more you blame yourself, the more you'll feel guilty about your child's ADHD, and the more your energy will be diverted away from helping your child and into futile self-punishment. It can sometimes be difficult to see how this dynamic works, as guilt pulls at your attention. The next exercises will help you discover how guilt and self-blame work against your efforts to help your child thrive.

EXERCISE: THE COSTS AND BENEFITS OF SELF-BLAME

What do you gain by blaming yourself? Consider all the ways you may benefit, then write them in a notebook. For example, perhaps by blaming yourself you feel like you are in control of the situation. Perhaps you feel less helpless by taking responsibility for the ADHD diagnosis. Try to generate as many possible benefits as possible. Ask yourself these prompting questions:

- What are the benefits for my child diagnosed with ADHD?

- What are the benefits to my spouse?

- What are the benefits to my other children?

- What are the benefits to my professional well-being?

- What are the benefits to my health?

Now consider the costs of self-blame, making a list in your notebook. The costs are all the negative impacts of blaming yourself. For example, perhaps you feel worse about yourself as a parent. Perhaps you spend valuable time ruminating about how have you failed your child. Perhaps you are afraid of interacting with your child for fear that you might make another mistake. Try to generate as many possible negative impacts of self-blame as possible. Ask yourself these questions:

- What are the costs for my child diagnosed with ADHD?

- What are the costs to my spouse?

- What are the costs to my other children?

- What are the costs to my professional well-being?

- What are the costs to my health?

Examine your list of costs and benefits for taking blame for your child's diagnosis. Most likely you have arrived at the conclusion that it is more to your benefit and your family's benefit for you to stop blaming yourself. Now, remember that your thoughts will ultimately change your feelings. Next time you find yourself feeling guilty or to blame, remind yourself that there are no substantial benefits and many costs to self-blame. Regardless of the truth or falsity of the charge, self-blame is simply not productive. One concrete way you can impact your child's transformation is to stop blaming yourself. This will help you gain control in a situation where you often find yourself feeling helpless.

EXERCISE: FACING YOUR WORST FEARS

If you find that no matter what you do, you cannot relieve yourself of feeling guilty, you can try this exercise:

1. Ask yourself the following question: If it is true that you are to blame for your child's ADHD, what is the worst thing that will happen? What is the worst result of this truth that you can imagine? What is the worst thing it could mean? Write your response in your notebook.

2. Look at your answer to this first question. Ask yourself, "If what I wrote in question 1 is true, then what is the worst thing that will happen?" For example, if you wrote, "If it's true that I'm responsible for causing my son's ADHD, then I'm a terrible mother," then you will want to ask yourself, "If I am a terrible mother, what is the worst thing that will happen?" Write your answer to this question in your notebook.

3. Look at what you have written in response to question 2. Now ask yourself what evidence you have that this conclusion is true. Write the evidence in your notebook.

4. Look at your response to question 2. Ask yourself what evidence you have that it is false. Write the evidence in your notebook.

You'll most likely find that your fears are essentially irrational with almost no evidence to support them. For example, if you asked yourself "What if it were true that I am a terrible mother?" and replied that you should have your children taken away from you, you would see how ridiculous your deepest fears are. Most likely you would find that there was no evidence to support that you would or should have your children taken from you. You will probably be able to generate a wealth of reasons for seeing why you are *not* a terrible mother. For example, you see that your child is healthy and happy despite her struggles with the diagnosis. You see that you love your child and that you both enjoy the time you spend together. Also, as you shift your understanding of ADHD from that of a disorder to a gift, you will begin to shift from taking the blame to taking the credit for having nurtured such a gifted, unique, and different child.

EXERCISE: GIVE YOURSELF CREDIT

Blaming yourself can become like a bad virus that spreads and infects the way you perceive everything else. You may be vulnerable to a tendency to see all the ways in which you are a failure as a parent. If you blame yourself, you may not be aware of and recognize all of the times you're a great parent. In order to counteract this tendency it is important to increase your awareness of your strengths as a parent. Try the following exercise:

1. Reflect over the past week. Write down all of the specific things you did as a parent that were loving and caring.

2. Complete the following sentence: My child is lucky to have me as a parent because . . .

3. As you move forward into this next week, keep a log of all the loving, caring, and helpful things you do, say, or think as a parent. You may want to buy a small notebook to keep with you so you don't forget any of your great parenting moments. Be sure to pay attention, looking for ways in which you give to your children, or sacrifice your own interests, or indulge your own interests so you'll have more to give your children. Be as specific, concrete, and thorough as possible. Do not leave anything out. Even if you find yourself thinking that you are grateful to be a parent, write that down—it counts.

Summary

In this chapter we reviewed some general strategies for beginning to transform your child's problems into strengths. The main techniques of cognitive behavioral therapy involve challenging negative thoughts, examining the evidence for negative expectations, generating positive expectations for you and your child, and reframing negative traits and expectations into positive traits and expectations. This chapter reviewed some general strategies that will guide you through many of the exercises in the rest of the book.

CHAPTER 3

Reclaiming Self-Esteem for Your Child

THE RISK TO SELF-ESTEEM

Self-esteem is your child's fundamental sense of being worthy, of deserving respect, and of respecting others. A child with a healthy sense of self-esteem does not feel less than other people, nor does he feel better than anyone else. Central to transforming your child's problems into strengths is that your child develop a realistic and positive sense of self-esteem. He needs to regain a sense that he is able to change outcomes in the world by changing his behavior. He needs to learn that he is powerful and not fundamentally flawed because of the diagnosis of ADHD. Your child needs to learn that he has much to offer his teachers, peers, siblings, and parents.

Because of both the insulting sound of the diagnosis of ADHD and the repeated failure experiences in school, your child's self-esteem is in double jeopardy. As a parent, it's important to be aware of these threats to your child's ability to feel good about himself and also his ability to believe that he should keep working hard to achieve his goals. You have the power to identify your child's tendency to believe that he cannot achieve his goals and to change those thoughts and beliefs. To help you in spotting this tendency, we will review threats to your child's self-esteem, not to scare you, but so you can look out for the signs that he may be losing confidence in himself and step in and help turn his thoughts around.

Sometimes children who feel bad about themselves will take on a sort of bravado and talk as if they are better than others. The hallmark of true self-esteem is respect for oneself and others. If your child does not have respect for himself, he will be impaired in social and academic settings. If he doesn't show respect for other children in an effort to protect himself from his own low feelings, he will have impaired social relationships.

Your child may feel inferior to other students because he often gets negative feedback from teachers and other students. He may feel inferior because he notices he is having a harder time succeeding than the other students. It may feel like schoolwork and behaviors such as sitting still come so much easier for others. It is easy for your child to make the leap to believing that he is somehow less than other students because of these difficulties. The loss of a sense of positive self-worth and the feeling of being inferior to others causes many behavioral disturbances and academic and social disturbances. The rest of this chapter will show how the loss of self-esteem creates symptoms that look like ADHD. As you can imagine, this dynamic can create a vicious cycle, such that the traits of ADHD lead to low self-esteem, which leads to increased severity of the traits, which then continues the cycle of lowering self-esteem. After showing how self-esteem is the fundamental building block in transforming your child's problems into strengths, we'll review a wide range of exercises for enhancing your child's self-esteem.

Self-Efficacy

While self-esteem reflects your child's felt sense of his general worth, self-efficacy reflects you child's specific beliefs about his ability to make changes in his life. Self-efficacy is a component of self-esteem. Your child's sense of self-efficacy is the set of beliefs and attitudes he has about his power to make his dreams come true. It means that he believes that if he wants to do better in school, he can work harder and do better. It means that if he wants to get along more smoothly with other students, he can try harder, learn social skills, and make friends. The opposite of self-efficacy is learned helplessness, when a person learns that their efforts don't achieve the intended results. If your child believes that no matter how hard he tries he won't do better in school, he will simply stop trying. If he believes that no matter what he does, he will never be popular with other students, he will act out aggressively toward others. After having respect for himself and others, the most important belief to instill in your child is that he can create and change his reality.

Children with ADHD are at risk for giving up, thereby making their symptoms worse. Researchers have shown that children with ADHD are less persistent in academic tasks than children who do not have this diagnosis (Hoza et al. 2001). They are less likely to persist in challenging activities, in part because they begin to believe that they do not have what it takes to succeed. This chapter will work toward showing how the diagnosis of ADHD creates or exacerbates some of its characteristic symptoms by lowering self-efficacy. Exercises in this chapter will help your child believe he has the power to create desired outcomes.

AVOIDING REJECTION: SELF-PROTECTIVE MEASURES

As we've seen, all of the traits of ADHD can be seen as differences rather than problems. But because these traits elicit rejecting responses from others, they get translated into problems that become more severe as the child's self-esteem falls. Your child's behavior has a certain logic to it. Much of his behavior can be seen as a predictable response of a sensitive child to an environment in which he has experienced repeated failures. Through accepted theories about how people learn and adapt, we know that people are motivated to avoid situations that are painful. If school has become painful and your child cannot simply leave the environment, he will adopt strategies for mentally leaving (inattention) or changing the environment in disruptive ways to express his anger and feelings of rejection.

By understanding your child's behavior as a strategy for coping with feelings of low self-esteem and low self-efficacy, you are empowered to transform your child. You can help your child by trying the following exercises to change his fundamental beliefs about who and how powerful he is.

Before we get to the exercises, let's take a brief look at how the specific symptoms of ADHD can be caused by low self-esteem and low self-efficacy. The symptoms listed below map onto the criteria used to make a diagnosis of ADHD.

Self-Handicapping: Response to Negative Feedback

Negative feedback may cause your child to give up trying or to self-handicap. Self-handicapping may be a strategy your child has developed to protect his self-esteem. This ineffective coping strategy can sometimes result from learned helplessness. If he can believe that he didn't really try when faced with failure, he can hold on to the possibility that he would do well if he did try. In the face of consistent and frequent negative feedback, children are likely to adopt self-defeating coping styles to protect some remnant of self-respect. Other symptoms of ADHD such as losing things, not following through on instructions, and becoming forgetful can also be seen as your child's strategy to protect himself through self-handicapping.

Difficulty Maintaining Attention and Following Through

As we'll discuss in later chapters, attention deficit is a social judgment and usually means that children are not focusing on what teachers and adults want them to pay attention to. Children are always paying attention to something, but it might be their own daydreams or the boy sitting next to them in class rather than the teacher's lessons. Although we'll reframe this trait as a strength later, it remains true that problematic aspects of this trait develop from feeling helpless to change the world.

If your child has given up hope that he can succeed through sustained effort, then often he will direct his attention toward other things. This is an effect of the "why try?" attitude that results from repeated failure. One of the most powerful instincts in humans and animals is to escape and avoid situations that are painful. If learning has become painful because it is associated with negative feedback, your child's inattention may be seen as a protective strategy.

Fidgeting

In later chapters, the way in which high energy levels can be understood as a strength will be reviewed. But this potential gift of exuberance can become problematic and disruptive for your child when he continually receives negative feedback. Hyperactivity may be a way for your child to avoid being mindful of his environment because it has become aversive or painful. Continually being "on the go" is a way of distracting himself from the awareness that he is not appreciated for who he is.

Somewhere within himself, your child knows that his differences represent a potential strength and that there is an injustice in the rejection he faces in the school system. As a child, he is not equipped to understand fully why he feels so rejected just for being himself. He protects himself from full awareness of these feelings by acting out and staying on the move. These symptoms are the opposite of mindfulness. Imagine how painful it would be for your child to be fully present to experience the rejection of the traits that are essential to who he is.

Disruptive Behavior and Impatience

While hyperactive behavior may be a way for your child to distract himself from the pain of his predicament, disruptive behavior is the expression of his anger at the injustice of the situation. If a child has repeatedly been told that his differences are a deficit and has come to believe that he is somehow inferior to his peers, he may be motivated to disrupt the environment out of a sense of anger. It's almost as if your child was saying, "If this environment rejects me, I'll show it!" Disrupting the classroom, teachers, and peers is a behavioral way of rejecting the environment first. This can be seen as a self-protective strategy.

ENHANCING SELF-ESTEEM

The main way to enhance your child's self-esteem will be to reframe the diagnosis of ADHD as a strength. Chapters 5 through 9 will detail the five gifts of ADHD and will reframe the symptoms as positive traits. The cornerstone of healing your child will be to convince him that his difference is a gift and not a "deficit disorder." In addition to changing both your and your child's vision of the diagnosis, there are many helpful techniques for increasing your child's sense of self-worth, challenging his self-defeating thoughts, and increasing his expectation for positive outcomes by changing his behavior.

It is also important that the self-esteem be realistic. You don't want to create illusory positive expectations for your child that will lead him to continued disappointment. The point is to keep your child's ability to persist intact, not to have him believe that he is better than others in any way. As mentioned earlier, sometimes children with ADHD adapt a bravado and overestimate their scholastic competence as a protective mechanism (Owens and Hoza 2003). If your child has an unrealistically positive sense of his academic performance, it may actually undermine his persistence on tasks. Actually, children may adopt this unrealistic belief in their achievement in order to justify not persisting. ADHD children who have consistent patterns of low achievement may tell their parents, "I don't need to study for the quiz. I know all the material, and I'll do great!" If this is the pattern your child displays, you will want to work toward increasing his sense of self-esteem and to increase a realistic sense of how much work he needs to do. The key is to increase persistence.

It is a truism that success is 99 percent hard work and 1 percent inspiration. Children with a diagnosis of ADHD have a harder time staying focused for long periods of time, have less motivation to try harder because they think they are handicapped, and may likely underestimate how much success is determined by persistent effort and hard work. Therefore, the following exercises will help your child address these differences so they do not become deficits.

EXERCISE: ACCEPTING THAT I AM DIFFERENT

In this exercise you will help your child to realistically accept that he's different. You will also guide him to have a compassionate response to this difference rather than getting mad at himself for being different.

1. Ask your child what having ADHD means to him. Let him talk as long or as little as he responds. Answer any questions, but try to get a sense of how he feels about the diagnosis. Turn this into a game by showing your child how he can use one of his hands to show you how his heart feels. Hold your hand out in a tight fist and say, "When someone tells me I did something wrong, my heart closes down and feels like this." Then, open your hand, facing up like you are holding a bowl and say, "When someone says I'm great just the way I am, my heart feels like this."

2. Now ask your child to show you with his hand how his heart feels when the teacher says he is disrupting class. If your child says he cannot do it or does not know how to tell what his heart is feeling, ask him to take a couple of breaths and concentrate on his heart area. If he continues to say he does not know what you want, tell him to just pretend. Remind him that there are no right or wrong answers, that this is just a game of pretend. After he shows you what his heart feels like by using his hand, ask him to show you what his heart feels like when the teacher says he is trying very hard and is pleased with him.

3. Now ask your child to show you with his hand how his heart feels when he hears that he has ADHD. He will probably have a closed fist. Ask him to tell you why his heart is closed and listen to his answer. Ask him what he needs to have happen to open his heart. Listen to him and make whatever changes are possible in the home and in the school setting.

4. Tell your child that ADHD is something that makes one different, but that differences are good and the difference of ADHD is a gift. Tell your child that he is different from other children and this sometimes makes life harder for him than for other children. Tell him that he can take two different attitudes toward having the diagnosis. He can be mad at others for not having the diagnosis and feel sorry for himself for having a diagnosis that makes him different, or he can realize how strong he is for having to make it through school when he is different from what the school expects of children. He can realize that his difference also is a gift, and that in some ways his traits make him really good at some things. His differences can serve the world in important, needed ways.

5. Ask your child to show you with his hand how each of these beliefs makes his heart feel. Likely he will show you that the first one makes his heart close and the second one makes his heart open. Tell him that he will want to focus on telling himself over and over the one that makes his heart open.

Rewarding Effort

One way to work toward increasing self-esteem realistically is to encourage your child to praise himself for making effort. If the child learns to reward himself for his efforts, his persistence will increase. If he praises himself only for successful outcomes, he might not have as much chance to reinforce himself in the beginning and may get frustrated. He may learn to value himself for outcomes rather than effort, which may in turn lead to negative thoughts about himself. Because your child's diagnosis is a difference that is at odds with current school settings, he needs to learn to reward himself based on efforts rather than outcomes.

EXERCISE: TRY-HARD BINGO CARD

You will also want to learn to reward your child for his efforts at improving his schoolwork, relationships with others, and behavior. You can do this by committing to noticing when he's trying and letting him know that you see his efforts. Give him verbal praise. On occasion, you can reward him with whatever goodies are motivating to him, whether it be a special snack, a dinner out at his favorite restaurant, or a trip to the park.

This strategy is an example of what's called *behavioral management*. Of all psychological theories about how to change people, behavioral management is acknowledged as the most effective way of transforming behaviors. Researchers have found that rewarding good behaviors increases them and punishing bad behaviors decreases those behaviors. This powerful strategy for change is effective with animals, little kids, the elderly, and almost any other population or culture you can imagine. For this exercise, focus on rewarding increased efforts. We will not have any exercises that use punishment of bad behavior. This is because, as they are rewarded, the positive behaviors become so prevalent that the bad behaviors eventually get edged out.

You can also make a game out of rewarding your child for making positive efforts. The following directions are for Try-Hard Bingo.

1. In your notebook, make a bingo card like the example on the next page. Tell your child that you will be playing a game of Try-Hard Bingo, in which he can get credit just for trying harder. Explain the rules of bingo, in this case that he will get a star if he can report one incidence of trying hard in one of the domains. Each day he will have a chance to earn stars. He wins if he gets a star in every domain on any one day or in one domain every day of the week. Each week you will want

to work out what the bingo prize will be for a day or a domain. For example, on any day that he shows that he tried hard in every domain, he gets to watch a half hour extra of TV, and for any domain that he shows that he tried hard every day of the week, he gets five dollars.

2. Keep a copy of the Try-Hard Bingo Card displayed prominently at home. Also give your child a copy to take to school with him. Ask him to try to be aware of every time that he tries harder to persist in schoolwork, to gain skills to get along with other children, or to manage his behavior when he doesn't feel like it. Ask him to write down how he tried and what he did and to put it under the right domain, schoolwork, relationships, or good behavior.

3. Every night spend some time filling out the Try-Hard Bingo Card. On any night that all three domains are checked off (you might want to use stickers or stars), make a big deal of giving your child the prize for that day. At the end of the week, determine if your child has won a domain bingo in schoolwork, good relationships, or good behavior. If so, offer lots of praise and the prize for that domain.

Try-Hard Bingo Card		
	Schoolwork	Good Relationships	Good Behavior
Monday			
Tuesday			
Wednesday			
Thursday			
Friday			
Saturday			
Sunday			

Here are some tips for making this game more successful: Spend a lot of time as you start out letting your child think about what good rewards would be. Let him make a long list and have long conversations about all the things he would like that would be pleasurable. Of course, you'll have to set limits. You wouldn't want your child to be allowed to eat pizza every night. But, within limits, agree on a wide range of rewards that are reasonable from your perspective and motivating for him. This will make the game fun for your child. By giving your child a lot of time to think about and talk about all the things he likes to have and to do, you'll make the game more fun. You might even come up with a reward scheme such that the Try-Hard Bingo Card for each week lists the reward for every possible bingo. For example, you might have a different reward for each day of the week and for each domain. In this way, your child's interest will be maintained, and he will be motivated each day of the week and in each domain.

CHANGE YOUR STATE, MAKE IT GREAT!

Often, low self-esteem results from children with the diagnosis of ADHD feeling that they are out of control of their lives. They can believe that their high energy and impulsiveness leave them with a devil-made-me-do-it attitude. They often have good intentions and feel out of control as they are called to account for their bad behavior. Low self-esteem may result also from being in a low mood, feeling blue about being out of control, or the cascade of negative feedback they get in school and from peers.

One of the quickest ways to give your child self-esteem is to show him that he is in charge of his own state. You can show him that no matter what happens, he can control his internal reactions and feelings. The quickest way for any person—adult or child—to change their state is to pay attention to their breathing. The second quickest way is to change body posture. The following exercises can be played as a game with your child to show him how he can change his mood in minutes.

EXERCISE: BE-A-BALLOON GAME

1. Before starting the game, ask your child how he feels on a scale of 1 to 10. Tell him that 1 means feeling pretty lousy and 10 means feeling awesome.

2. Remind your child of the balloons he has seen in parades, such as Underdog in the Macy's Thanksgiving Day Parade or any other inflatable toy he may have seen. Tell him to sit in a chair and pretend that he is Underdog on the day before the Thanksgiving day parade. He is just a balloon with no air in him yet. You can demonstrate by sitting in a chair with your arms, shoulders, and head hanging down. You can also say you feel like you are a rag doll, all loose and heavy.

3. Ask him to take in a deep breath and imagine that he is being filled with air and is expanding. You will want to play along with him and demonstrate. As you are being filled with air, stick out your chest, raise your hands in the air as if they are being filled with air, and raise your head up. Imagine an inflatable person being filled with air, and tell your child to imagine this also. When your child is "fully inflated," say "Hold it for one . . . two . . . three and blow out all your breath" making a "whewww" sound, as if air is being let out of a balloon. Tell your child that when you say release, he is to let out his breath and to collapse again in a relaxed, loose, and heavy position.

4. Practice this exercise two more times. After doing it three times, ask your child how he feels now on a scale of 1 to 10, with 1 being pretty lousy and 10 being awesome. It is likely that he will feel better and the number will be higher than the one that you started with. Point out to your child how his number went higher and how he was able to make that happen just by breathing and changing his posture.

5. Show your child how he can do this anytime in a smaller way, without pretending to be a parade balloon. Show him how to take a deep breath, hold it for a count of three, and release.

He can do this anytime he feels anxious, upset, or has hurt feelings. This exercise will show him that he's in control of his state. Also show him that he can raise his head and hold his shoulders back, and that just this change will improve his mood and cause others to respond to him in a more positive way.

EXERCISE: ACT LIKE YOUR FAVORITE SUPERSTAR

This exercise will tap into your child's imagination, which can seem to be on overdrive all the time, and channel it to help him change to a positive state of mind. Like the preceding exercise, the important point is to learn that he can—through simple and quick games—change his emotional state very quickly. Through these skills, he will learn that he is in charge, and that other people cannot control him.

Sometimes parents get worried when their child has a seeming obsession with a sports star, a movie star, a film or book character, or a mythical character. However, usually these preoccupations are an attempt at self-healing for your child. The superstar your child has latched onto can be used as an inspiration and motivational force. Also, you can use your child's preoccupation with this person to engage his interest in exercises to help transform his problems into strengths. While your child will not likely be motivated to engage in a behavioral management program per se, any game that involves his superstar person or character will provide a lot of energy and motivation for the exercise. In this way, the game provides one more arena where you don't have to be working against your child, but rather with his own set of intense interests.

Of course, you will have to use your judgement when using this exercise. Typically, children's superstars are characters like Harry Potter, sports figures like Barry Bonds, or mythical figures like knights in shining armor. If for some reason your child's hero is more along the lines of a villain-type figure, you may want to move on to another exercise. Throughout this book you will be given more than enough exercises for each problem you're trying to transform. Do not push an exercise if your child doesn't like it, you don't like it, or it doesn't fit for some reason. If your child responds to only a handful of the exercises presented in this book, you will still see dramatic changes that will stop the vicious cycle of his spinning out of control.

1. It is best to demonstrate this exercise when your child is upset, angry, or hurt. You'll want to demonstrate his power to change his state. Say, "Let me show you who is in control of how you feel. Tell me on a scale of 1 to 10, with 1 being terrible and 10 being awesome, how you feel right now."

2. Tell him to think of his favorite superstar and to hold a posture like that character or person. If it's a book or movie character, ask for a moment or scene that is particularly heroic. Tell your child to stand like the superstar, pretend like he is that superstar, and feel all the feelings of that superstar. Tell him that for the next two minutes he should walk, talk, and act like the superstar.

3. After two minutes, ask your child how he feels different. Ask him how he feels using the 1-to-10 scale. Likely he will have changed his feelings, thoughts, and attitudes just by pretending to be his favorite superstar.

HELPING YOUR CHILD RECLAIM CONTROL

Children who are given the diagnosis of ADHD have a more difficult time controlling their behavior than other children. It often seems that words and behaviors fly out that were never processed by any central organizing system. This lack of filtering leads to inappropriate behaviors that are disruptive to others.

To make matters worse, sometimes the diagnosis of ADHD, because it sounds like a medical disorder, increases your child's belief that he cannot control his own behavior. It is almost as if the ADHD diagnosis gives permission to your child to act out and justification for bad behavior once it's occurred. Instead of "the devil made me do it," the diagnosis may lead to a my-ADHD-made-me-do-it attitude.

Feeling like you can control your behavior, your thoughts, and your attitudes is a central component of self-esteem. In addition to behavioral management strategies, your child needs to believe that he is capable of controlling his actions. The following pretend game will help your child reclaim his belief in his own power.

EXERCISE: THE COACH AND THE CHEERLEADER

Set up this exercise by telling your child that, like any super sports star, he needs to have a coach and a cheerleader to do his best. Tell him that you want to play a pretend game with him where he learns to be his own coach and cheerleader. Any toys or props you can get to make the game more fun will help. You could make a bullhorn out of paper for the cheerleader, or make some pom-poms. For the coach you could get a baseball cap or a toy whistle. Costumes and props will make the game more appealing to your child. If there is a specific team, sport, or player that your child is enamored of, a team jersey can make this exercise come alive.

Start by asking your child to tell you how a coach and a cheerleader help sports players. Generate as many answers as possible. You will want to make sure to include the following points:

- A coach tells players how handle certain problems during a game.

- A coach makes the player practice, practice, practice.

- A coach tells the player what to expect.

- A coach gives the player strategies to prepare for game day.

- A coach will give pep talks to players.

- A coach will challenge the player if they have wrong ideas.

- A cheerleader gives a lot of support to the players.

- A cheerleader says nice things to the players.

- A cheerleader keeps hope up when the team is not winning the game.

- A cheerleader never gives up on the team.

Pick a recent concrete problem and show your child how to be a cheerleader or coach. For example, if in school the week before your son got in trouble for hitting his pencil against his desk and disrupting class, that would be a good place to start. Following is an example of how to do this.

Mom: What did you say to yourself when the teacher asked you to stop hitting the desk with your pencil?

Marty: I told the teacher I was trying, but I said to myself that I couldn't stop. I didn't know what else to do with myself.

Mom: Okay, I'm going to pretend like I'm a cheerleader.
(Mom takes out paper bullhorn she made with Marty in preparation for the exercise). Go Marty, You can do it.
Yes you can! You can stop if you want. You have the power, Marty. If you try hard, you can do anything you want! Now (putting on a coach's baseball hat and blowing a toy whistle) I'm going to be the coach. The coach says, "Hey Marty, in order to win this game you can take a deep breath, you can calm down. Try taking a couple of deep breaths and relax. That will help you win the game. Act like you're a rag doll, and go limp. Let your body relax, feel heavy and warm. Remember to breathe!" Okay, how do you feel now?

Marty: I feel better. I feel like, if I tried, I could do better in class.

The next step is to reverse roles. You act out the same problematic behavior and your son pretends to be the coach and the cheerleader. The following is an example of how to do this.

Mom: Okay, I'm Marty, and I'm in class. (Mom has fun pretending to be Marty, sits down with a pencil, and begins hitting it against a table.) Why's everyone looking at me and why's that teacher telling me to quiet down and stop hitting my pencil on the desk? I like the noise, it helps me calm down. It's so boring in here! I can't stop anyway—I have ADHD.

Marty: Hey Marty, you can do it. You can stop if you want. Why don't you calm down by taking a deep breath. You can do the balloon exercise and fill yourself up with air. That would be another way to calm down. Go Marty! You can do it!

Mom: But that teacher is so mean to me. If I stop, she wins. She embarrassed me in front of the whole class.

Marty: Hey Marty, you win if you stop hitting the pencil, because then you show that you can control yourself. Don't let the teacher bring you down. Focus on you. You can do it. You can control yourself.

Mom: Great job being coach and cheerleader, Marty!

Tell your son that he can be the cheerleader and the coach for himself, any day and time he needs a coach or cheerleader. Tell him that everybody needs both a coach and a cheerleader with them at all times, but that he has to be that for himself.

Get out three-by-five cards and create coach and cheerleader cards. Be very creative in making the cards. Use stickers, markers, and crayons so that the cards are fun to make and fun to look at. This is a project that will be fun to do with your son. On one side, the card should say "Coach" or "Cheerleader." On the other side you should write a statement to help your child believe he can control his behavior or a specific strategy. Some examples of coach cards are below:

- Stay in the game! Keep trying!

- You win if you keep trying!

- Take a deep breath and calm down!

- Stay focused!

- Pretend like you're a rag doll. Feel your body as warm and heavy. This will help you sit still.

Some examples of Cheerleader cards are these:

- You can do it!

- You have the power! Try harder!

- Keep going! Keep trying!

- You can control your behavior!

- You are in charge!

- You win if you control your actions!

Your child can take these cards to school with him to teach him how to talk to himself. The cards will be more effective if they are specific to particular problems. For example, if the teacher repeatedly complains that your son cannot sit still, you can create cheerleader cards that say, "I can sit still."

Summary

This chapter offered many different strategies for helping your child improve his self-esteem and his ability to try harder in managing his behavior in school settings and in relationships. Remember that if you or your child don't like any of the exercises, it's best not to push these games. They will only work if you and your child have fun with them. You don't need to do every exercise to transform your child. If only one or two of these games works well for both you and your child, it is better to do that exercise repeatedly. Remember also that the more creative and fun you can be in making these games rather than tasks or chores, the more success you will have. Your child has an immense capacity for imagination, and the more you rely on using that imagination in pretend games rather than on moralizing about the right way to behave, the more you will engage your child's attention. You will also be building a strong relationship with him that will become the foundation for transforming his problems into strengths.

CHAPTER 4

How to Become Your Child's Advocate, Not Apologist

The key ingredient in transforming your child's diagnosis into a gift is your relationship with her. What your child needs more than anything is for you to be on her side. After that, what your child needs is for you to try to get her teachers and mental-health-care professionals on her side. In short, your child needs you to become her advocate.

BARRIERS TO BECOMING AN ADVOCATE

Advocating for your child may have been difficult for you to do up until now. This chapter offers exercises that will make this easier for you to do and specific strategies for improving your effectiveness. It is important that you not blame yourself for how you have interacted with your child in the past. It's also important that you not beat yourself up for the times that you've failed to move forward. Many things may have stood in the way of you becoming a forceful advocate, and many parents feel all too ready to take on guilt about their kid's struggles. To help relieve some of this self-blame and remind you of the real challenges you've been facing, we will review the significant barriers that may have made it difficult for you act as your child's advocate.

More Than a Handful

The first barrier that's probably made it difficult for you to become your child's advocate is that your child really is a handful. In fact, your child is most likely more than a handful. All young children have a lot of energy and are rambunctious compared to their parents and teachers. Part of the gift of ADHD is that your child really does have even more energy than a typical child. In some ways, your child is like a 50-watt lightbulb that has 100 watts of energy coursing through her.

Your child has a hard time managing her own high levels of energy. As a parent, you don't have an enormous amount of energy but still have to manage not only your child's high levels of energy but also her difficulties managing the energy herself. In short, children with ADHD can be exhausting for adults. Out of sheer fatigue, you may have found yourself short-tempered with your child. Or you may have found yourself using strategies to control her that you know are not helpful in the long run.

Because you may have your own complaints about how to manage such a live wire, you may have become an apologist for your child in interacting with others, including teachers. For example, when the teacher complains about your child's behavior you may have found it easy to apologize to the teacher. You may feel guilty, thinking that your child's teacher considers you a bad parent, so you have to show him how nice you are by apologizing for your child. Your own exhaustion and frustration are probably one of the barriers you have faced to becoming an advocate for your child. Later in this chapter we will review why, although you may be sympathetic with complaints about your child, you will need to gently challenge them.

Iron-Clad Authority

Another barrier you may face is your own perception or misperception that teachers and mental-health-care professionals are iron-clad authorities. If the teacher is complaining that your child is a problem, you may think, "She must be right. After all, she sees lots of children and has a lot of points of comparison." If a mental-health-care professional tells you that your child is disturbed, you may think, "He knows what he's talking about. He has studied this and is an expert on child behavior." In both of these cases, you are misguided about the authority you give to these experts' perceptions. In addition, even if they were right, your conceding to their authority is not helpful to your child.

One of the reason these authorities are wrong about your child is that they are almost certainly working from a different paradigm. It doesn't matter how much knowledge or experience a person has—if they're working from a different worldview, then they will not be the best judge of your child's behavior. For example, for many years the world's greatest astronomy experts looked at the skies with the understanding that the earth was the center of the universe. Although they were the experts, their fundamental worldview was wrong, and therefore they made many mistakes in their judgments. Similarly, this book offers a paradigm shift—or change in worldview—suggesting that ADHD is not a disorder but rather a gift.

If you can overcome the barrier of seeing teachers and other professionals as authorities, you can begin to advocate for your child by showing people how to see your child as you do. It may help you to remember that these experts may be right about the details, but they are wrong about their grand vision. For example, your child may jump out of her seat a lot during the school day and may interrupt other students. But taken together, these behaviors don't have to be seen as indicating that your child is fundamentally disturbed. As you shift your own vision of your child, you can learn to help others who are involved in your child's life shift their view and so better serve your child.

Conflict Avoidance

You may also have hesitated to advocate for your child because you were afraid of being thought of as adversarial or oppositional—the very same words sometimes used to describe your child.

Many people find it very difficult to confront others with a view-point that challenges what the other person is saying. Almost every-one is uncomfortable with disagreement. And many of us have a tendency to exaggerate our fears in our mind. For example, if your child's teacher says that your daughter is lazy, as an apologist, you will apologize profusely to the teacher and promise to instill even stricter controls to keep your child on top of her homework. In contrast, as an advocate for your child, you might say that you do not experience your child as lazy. Rather, she is very creative and you have noticed that she often becomes absorbed in drawing projects and is capable of intense effort when working on them.

As you imagine becoming an advocate for your child you may become fearful that the teacher will get angry at you for contradicting him. You may be fearful that he will think you are just being difficult, and no wonder your child is such a problem. You may even worry that he will be mad and take it out on your child. Or you may wonder if the teacher will think you are just out of touch with reality. With practice, you will find that many of your fears are unfounded. Try the following exercise for coping with these concerns.

EXERCISE: CHALLENGING YOUR FEARS OF BEING CHALLENGING

1. In your journal or notebook, write down your major concerns about reframing your child's behavior to a complaining teacher. For example, you may be afraid that your child's teacher will think you are a bad parent.

2. Using a scale of 1 (very unlikely) to 10 (very likely), write down an estimate about the likelihood that your fear will actually happen.

3. Now write down thoughts that contradict your fear. Include all the positive things that may result from confronting your child's teacher. For example, if you are afraid that your child's teacher will think you're a bad parent, you could write down that he actually might think you are a good parent for having such a positive view of your child. Or maybe your child's teacher would see that you were right, that your child has many positive traits that he didn't notice. He might even start to give your child more positive attention in class.

4. Write down strategies you could use to cope if your fear did come true; for example, if your child's teacher said to you, "No wonder your child is so difficult. It's obvious you are overprotective of her and oppositional to boot." In writing down coping strategies, you might write down specific responses, such as "Your comments are insulting and not helpful to my child or my efforts to advocate that she get the best education possible. Let's stay focused on what we can do to help my child." Other coping strategies involve what you would say to yourself. For example, if your daughter's teacher did say such a thing, you would be right to have serious con- cerns about your daughter having such an insulting teacher. You might say to yourself, "No wonder my child is having so many problems in school—her teacher really is mean and intolerant." You might also want to write down strategies for solving this problem. If your daughter's teacher really is so insensitive, you might want to find ways to get her out of his classroom.

5. After going through these exercises, set up a time to meet with one of your child's teachers who has given you negative feedback. Share with this teacher your different vision of your child. Emphasize your goal to become an advocate for your child so that she will receive the best care possible. Affirm to the teacher that you are certain that he has the same goals to

serve your child, but that you may have different views about the nature of your child's behaviors.

6. After returning from your visit with the child's teacher, evaluate your original fears. Write down all of the positive things that came from the meeting. Write down all of the outcomes that you hope will happen. For example, you might write that the teacher really seemed interested in your perspective on your child and that he did not get offended when you challenged his perspective. You might also write down that you are hopeful that he will begin to see your child as gifted and give her more positive attention, helping your daughter to improve in that class.

THE IMPORTANCE OF BECOMING AN ADVOCATE

Having reviewed why you might have had a difficult time in the past becoming an advocate for your child, you can let yourself off the hook. You can also be gentle with yourself as you move into this new role. In this section, we turn to the reasons for why it is so important that you become your child's advocate. By becoming her advocate you address the fundamental cornerstones of transforming your child's problems into strengths—your relationship with your child, your child's environment, and your child's self-esteem.

Starting a Synergistic Cycle

By becoming an advocate for your child, you start a synergistic cycle that transforms symptoms into talents—or at the least, lovable eccentricities. *Synergistic* means that small changes will work together to create larger changes. A small change in direction can set off a cycle that leads to more and more positive changes. This can work against the vicious cycle that easily develops when negative views are taken of your child's symptoms. The synergistic cycle is made up of the following factors:

1. As you advocate for your child, you feel empowered and maintain your positive view of her.

2. As you feel better about yourself and your child your interactions with her are loving and rewarding for both of you.

3. As your child feels loved and rewarded, she tries to show love through increased efforts at home and at school.

4. As your child tries harder at school, she begins to experience more positive feedback.

5. As she interacts with you in more loving ways, you find it easier to maintain your positive view and loving interactions.

6. Finally, the result of this synergistic cycle is that you and your child have a loving, close, connected relationship in which you work together and are on each other's side.

There will be a strong link between how supported your child feels by you and how hard she will try to work toward the goals that you and she collaboratively set. The more you and your child work together, the more she will transform before your eyes. Also, by becoming an advocate for your child, you will feel empowered. The more empowered you feel, the more capable you are of connecting with your child. It is human nature that if you feel hopeless to change your child, you will feel like you are failing her. This perceived failure will make you feel anxious and guilty. These feeling will prove to be a barrier to connecting with your child. If every time you think of her you feel anxious and guilty, you will find it difficult to create the intimacy you both crave. The more empowered you feel to help your child, the easier it will be to create the connection you want.

Also, by becoming an advocate for your child and offering teachers some alternatives and ideas, you will refocus your own energy in the direction that is most helpful for your child—on the parent-child bond. In the face of negative feedback from teachers, parents too easily worry that they'll be seen as bad parents or that they actually are bad at parenting. Spending your time worrying about whether or not you are perceived as a bad parent should not be the focus of your time and energy. In fact, worrying about what other parents, teachers, or health-care providers think of you will act as a barrier to being the good parent that you really are! As you practice becoming an advocate for your child, you will realize that rather than directing your behavior and energy toward creating the impression that you are a good parent, you can defend your child and challenge other people's perceptions.

The opposite to the synergistic cycle is the vicious cycle. The vicious cycle that is set up by being an apologist for your child looks like this:

1. You apologize for your child's behavior after a teacher gives you negative feedback.

2. By accepting this negative feedback, you begin to see your child as essentially flawed.

3. You feel like you must have done something wrong and feel worse about yourself as a parent.

4. You are more likely to become angry or frustrated with your child.

5. As your child gets negative feedback from you and feels a lack of closeness, she behaves in problematic ways to express her own distress.

6. The more your child acts in problematic ways, the more negative feedback she gets at school, and the more frustrated you feel.

7. The more frustrated you feel, the more difficult it is to feel connected to your child.

8. You and your child both feel a growing distance between the two of you, and you begin to feel helpless and hopeless.

Becoming an advocate for your child means not accepting other people's negative evaluations of her. In addition, you tactfully offer an alternative way of understanding your child to the teacher or health-care professional. Below is an example of a dialogue in which the parent acts as an advocate.

Teacher: Ms. Jones, thank you for taking the time to meet with me. As we discussed on the phone, Andrea has been a problem in class. She just doesn't seem to pay attention, and she acts out by telling jokes to the boys in class during classroom exercises. This behavior is typical of ADHD students, and you should know that your daughter's behavior is out of control. Every time she does this, I have had to stop class and tell her to sit in her seat and refrain from disturbing the whole class. After I warn her, her behavior seems to get worse. On occasion she's even insulted other kids in the class.

Ms. Jones: Mr. Welch, thank you for your involvement with my daughter. I appreciate your concern for her well-being and development. I, too, want the best for her and want her to benefit from all that you have to offer students. I'm very close with my daughter, and I've noticed that recently she has become interested in boys in a different way than she has before. I think what you're describing is her first awkward attempts at flirting. I wonder if, when you stop class and single her out, she feels embarrassed. I'm guessing that she probably doesn't want the class to think she's flirting, so she then tries to prove she doesn't like the boys by acting insulting toward them. Maybe you could try pulling her aside privately before class and telling her that the best way to impress cute boys is to make them think you're smart. In my experience, Andrea responds very well to coaching and gets embarrassed very easily. I wonder if you could try this approach and see if it works. It might be that singling her out in class is making her behavior worse. It seems worth a try.

Teacher: Hmm, I've never thought of it that way. I understand your child has a diagnosis of ADHD, and this behavior seems like it's out of control. I can try what you're suggesting and see how it works. I'll take her aside privately from now on. Thanks for your suggestion. We'll see how it works.

When Ms. Jones gets home, she feels empowered that she challenged the teacher respectfully, and she shares with her husband that she thinks Andrea is becoming interested in boys. They chuckle and decide it might be time for Mom to have a talk with Andrea about boys. Ms. Jones tells Andrea she had the chance to talk to her teacher, Mr. Welch, that she told him that she knows Andrea doesn't like to be embarrassed in front of the whole class, and that Mr. Welch agreed not to do that anymore. Andrea feels important because her mom stood up for her to her teacher and resolves to make Mom proud of her by trying hard in Mr. Welch's class.

As you can see from this dialogue, by becoming an advocate for your child, you work to develop a positive interpretation of behaviors. In so doing you can change others' perceptions of your child and your own emotional reactions to her will be more positive. As you practice this, you will also feel more empowered. You won't spend your time worrying if others think you are a bad parent—you will address the issue head-on and challenge it.

In contrast, the vicious cycle of being an apologist for your child can look like the following.

Teacher: Ms. Jones, thank you for taking the time to meet with me. As we discussed on the phone, Andrea has been a problem in class. She just doesn't seem to pay attention and acts out by telling jokes to the boys in class during classroom exercises. This behavior is typical of ADHD students, and you should know your daughter's behavior is out of control. Every time she does this, I have had to stop class and tell her to sit in her seat and refrain from disturbing the whole class. After I warn her, her behavior seems to get worse. On occasion she's even insulted other kids in the class.

Ms. Jones: Mr. Welch, I'm so sorry that Andrea is acting out in class again. We're doing everything we can to help her. After I got your call, I called the psychiatrist. Maybe we can increase her medication. We're doing everything we can at home, but we're just at our wits' end.

Teacher: Well, I'm glad that you've made an appointment to check with the psychiatrist. Her behavior is disrupting the whole class and making my job nearly impossible.

Ms. Jones: (embarrassed, feeling like a bad parent) I'm so sorry. We will do everything we can at home to get her not to act out in class. I will be sure to tell her that she is disrupting your class and let her know that there will be serious consequences if she doesn't start behaving in school. In fact, I will tell her that if I get one more phone call from Mr. Welch, she'll have to miss a softball game.

Teacher: Well, thank you Ms. Jones. I need as much support from parents in the home as I can get in order to manage ADHD students. I'm glad we're on the same page.

Ms. Jones goes home feeling helpless and like a bad mom. She feels out of control and frustrated that no matter what she does Andrea doesn't seem to change. She goes home and gives Andrea a stern warning about what will happen if she continues to act out in Mr. Welch's class. Andrea feels confused about why she can't seem to control her behavior and feels all alone because her mom is mad at her. She doesn't know who to turn to and doubts that she can control her own behavior. That night she plays too rough with her little sister and gets in trouble again. She wonders "Why can't I be good like my sister? No one gets mad at her." She says to herself, "I guess I just can't do anything right."

In this dialogue, you can see how apologizing for your child's behavior sets a vicious cycle in motion that affects the whole family. Ms. Jones feels bad about herself and so does Andrea. They get pushed further and further apart as they both conclude that they're failures. Andrea is frustrated that her mom doesn't support her, and Ms. Jones is frustrated that Andrea can't control her behavior. Both feel increasingly helpless.

It is also important to note that children find it very difficult to articulate their own feelings, even to themselves. Children generally act out feelings. In this way, bad feelings lead to bad behavior. The example above illustrates how negative feedback about behavior serves to increase the very behavior that is problematic. Teachers tend to focus on the bad behavior as evidence of the diagnosis of ADHD. The diagnosis also makes it more likely that a teacher will give negative feedback rather than trying to understand other reasons for the behavior.

As you can see from these two vignettes, becoming an advocate for your child gives you the potential to change the environment she experiences at school. By reframing your child's behaviors and traits, you may enlist teachers to shift their perspective and try out behaviors that are less discouraging to your child. Similarly, in addition to enhancing your relationship with her, you will improve her self-esteem just by becoming an advocate. Children internalize their parents' attitudes toward them. When you show your child that you are willing to go out on a limb to defend her, she knows she is worthwhile and works hard to demonstrate to you and the teachers that you are right to defend her. She will feel safe, protected, and loved. All of these lead to feelings of self-worth and a determination to prove you right and the teachers wrong.

CONSTRUCTING GOOD BEHAVIOR

One of the most effective ways to encourage good behavior in your child is to continually construct interpretations that her existing behavior is already good behavior. Or, you can at least tell yourself and your child ways in which her behavior is meaningful or makes sense in some way. For example, in the case of Andrea and Mr. Welch, the parent suggested to the teacher that her daughter's behavior was simply awkward flirting rather than a pernicious symptom of ADHD. This ability to interpret your child's behavior as having a nonpathological meaning will serve your child in many ways and will serve your relationship with her. In some ways, more than anything else in the world, that is what your child wants and needs—for you to be on her side.

As you demonstrate powerfully that you are her advocate, she will internalize the ability to reframe her self-understandings in positive ways. This ability is the basis of self-esteem. In addition, she will internalize the ability to defend and protect herself. This skill will serve her in two ways: first, she will be able to soothe herself, and second, she'll be able to stand up for herself. These abilities will become a foundation of her ability to create positive mood states and to change her internal state in the face of negative feedback.

These abilities will serve a protective function against the tendency to use drugs and alcohol. Children with ADHD are at increased risk for drug and alcohol abuse (Barkley 2000). One reason for the increased risk is that these substances are used to soothe the negative emotions that result from frequent experiences of rejection and failure. To the extent that your child has coping skills to protect herself from negative moods, she will be less at risk for using and abusing drugs and alcohol.

The following exercise will encourage you to search for positive explanations for your child's behavior. This will help you become an articulate advocate for your child. It will also help you to teach your daughter how to do this for herself. This practice becomes very important, because the diagnosis of ADHD has a tendency to make all of the child's behavior seem to others like it is part of a deficit or disorder. In fact, much of your child's behavior may not be related to the diagnosis of ADHD at all. And even the behavior that is related to this difference can be reframed to show how it represents a gift.

EXERCISE: STORYTELLING

1. Spend a week observing your own reactions to your child's behavior or reports of her behavior from school. In this week, keep a journal of these reactions and thoughts. Write down the behavior that you observed or what the teacher said about your child. Then record the story that you tell yourself about your daughter. For example, Mr. Welch, your child's teacher, may have called to tell you that your daughter seems to be daydreaming throughout much of class, and when she's called on, makes it clear that she wasn't paying attention. Then write down your thoughts about what you've heard. So in our

example you'd write, "When Mr. Welch told me about Janet's daydreaming in class, I felt frustrated with her. Why can't she just pay attention like all the other kids? Maybe she isn't as smart as the other kids. Maybe her ADHD is a progressive disorder and she's going to continue to get worse. She might fail a grade or just drop out of school when she's sixteen. How is she going to make it in the world if she can't get good grades in school? She's going to be shut out from all the opportunities for higher education and making a career for herself."

2. After one week of just recording events and your reactions, purposefully change the stories you tell yourself. Search for positive interpretations of your child's behavior. Write down a story that makes your child's behavior meaningful and positive. Create happy endings. It doesn't matter if the story is true. For now, just practice telling yourself good stories with positive endings. What we know is that these stories can become self-fulfilling prophesies by creating positive outcomes for your child. So for now just create stories that frame your child in positive ways. For example, after Mr. Welch complains about Janet's daydreaming, a good story would be, "Today, after Mr. Welch called to complain about Janet daydreaming in class, I was really frustrated with Mr. Welch. What's wrong with that man? Of course Janet is daydreaming in his class. She is very creative and imaginative. I bet she was so excited about what Mr. Welch was talking about ten minutes earlier that she reflected deeply about the class material and went off on a line of thought that was original. Maybe I can teach Janet to share with Mr. Welch and the class that she was thinking about the material and share what she was thinking. Maybe if Janet can share her process, Mr. Welch will gain an appreciation for her curiosity and how reflective and imaginative she is. Some day Janet will make brilliant creative contributions to whatever field she goes into because of her powerful imagination." Generate as many positive stories as you can.

3. With this reframing in your mind, ask your daughter directly what was going on for her in the event described by the teacher. Listen carefully to your child. If she offers a

meaningful explanation for her behavior, accept it and incorporate it into your story. Keep in mind that often children aren't able to articulate their inner process clearly. They may just feel confused and not have a good understanding of what happened or why it happened. You can offer the positive stories you generated to your child and see what seems right to her. You may be surprised to find that your child says, "Yes, that's exactly what happened. I was so flustered by getting in trouble that I forgot I had been thinking about the material presented earlier in class. How did you know?"

This exercise will help you to become an advocate for your child. It will also bring you closer to your child by giving you the chance to listen to her explanation of her behavior rather than having a knee-jerk reaction that she must be doing something wrong. You must be prepared for the likelihood that your child will not have a good explanation. For this reason, it's helpful for you to generate positive stories and share these with your child for her to explore as possibilities. By sharing your positive stories, you can stop the vicious interpersonal cycle that can result between parents and children diagnosed with ADHD. As you generate a positive synergistic cycle, you are well on your way to transforming your child's problems into strengths.

EXERCISE: THE APPLE DOESN'T FALL FAR FROM THE TREE

One way to help you to generate positive stories for your child is to explore ways in which you have some similarities to her problematic behavior. Through the power of nature or nurture, there are very likely some similarities between your child's "bad" behavior and your own history or ways of being in the world. Sometimes you may think you're the opposite of your child. Even if this is the case, try to find memories of times when you acted similarly to the behavior your child gets in trouble for. Sometimes parents who have worked hard to overcome tendencies to goof off, act out, or rebel have moved in the opposite direction by becoming overly controlled. Sometimes it's obvious how much like your child you are, but you have exerted enormous discipline to overcome your own difficulties in paying attention or behaving appropriately.

1. Assign yourself one half hour a day for one week just to think about how you are like your child. Write in your journal specific memories or events where you acted like your child, or got in trouble in the same way your child gets in trouble. For example, maybe you remember that your freshman year in college you failed two classes because you just weren't interested in your classes and wanted to explore your newfound independence. Maybe you remember the time you got in trouble at school because you insulted another student. Remember why you did what got you in trouble. Looking back, try to understand why you acted the way in which you did. Reflect on how you understood it at that time compared to how you understand it now. One parent remembered having been dragged to the principal's office for having hit another student. She remembered being mystified about why she had done this. She couldn't explain to herself or the principal why she hit the student. As the parent remembered this incident, she realized that she had just had significant losses in her family at the time she got in trouble. She realized that no one talked to her about how she was feeling, and she must have been taking it out on this other student at school. Of course, when she was in sixth grade she could not explain why she hit the student. As an adult, it was obvious to her why this had happened.

2. Write in your journal your own reflections about behaviors you share or have shared in your past with your child. Try to see how explanations similar to those for your own behavior may be impacting your child. For example, the mother who remembered hitting another student realized that maybe her daughter had some feelings of loss around the fact that her husband had recently lost his job and seemed depressed. Maybe her daughter needed to talk about the dramatic changes in the family.

3. Take action on any insights that emerge. For example, talk to your child about any recent losses or stresses in the family. Make sure she has a chance to talk about any feelings of sadness, anger, or fear that she may feel in response to these events in the family. Your child is very sensitive, and you may have felt that by not talking about recent stressors you were protecting your child. Usually, your child will be made even more anxious by silence around significant changes. The more open you can be in talking about your own feelings and reactions, the more your child will benefit. Even if your own reactions are negative, your child will only feel connected to you if you genuinely share your reactions. Because children diagnosed with ADHD are particularly sensitive to reading when people are being insincere, your daughter will be disturbed by any perception that you're not being straight with her, and she will tend to think that things are worse than they really are. For example, if the mother in the example shares with her child that she is worried about Dad and that they both have some anxieties about his not having a job at the time, your child will actually feel relieved and connected to you. Your child will feel relieved because she probably sensed the tension all along, and now she has a validation of these feelings. And she now also has a chance to share her own anxieties. Your child will also feel closer to you because you're being honest and authentic. Of course, you want to be both honest and protective. This means revealing your fears, sadness, and anger but also reassuring her that many resources are available and that while this is a difficult time, you are certain to make it through.

4. If it is appropriate, you should share with your child your own previous life stories that are similar to what she is going through. This will help you to connect with your child and show her how one can overcome difficulties. You should also share what you did to turn your situation around or what you wish you would have done to turn things around sooner. These stories will help your child feel less alone and more supported. This will help her get through difficult times.

Summary

The main point of this chapter was to remind you that what your child wants and needs more than anything in the world is a close connection to you. Your child's relationship with you will be the cornerstone for turning her problems into strengths.

CHAPTER 5

The Gift of Creativity

AN ESSENTIAL OPENNESS

In this chapter we begin to reframe the specific symptoms of ADHD in terms of specific gifts. We will review how your child's spaciness, distractibility, and impulsiveness are essential attributes for promoting creativity. Fire needs oxygen to shine and burn. Similarly, creative genius or inspiration requires a certain sort of openness, exactly the sort of openness your child displays. Creativity often requires reframing or rethinking old problems. Openness, or the more negative term of "spaciness," provides a larger frame for seeing a bigger picture, allowing for space to solve old problems. Many people have said that insanity is trying to solve problems with the same level of thinking that created the problem. Spaciness lends itself to a different level of thought than that which typically creates most problems. Thus, children with ADHD who have been labeled as spacy often have the capacity to solve problems created by rigid modes of thinking. Daydreaming is the fount of creativity in that it is essentially the process of engaging the imagination. Imagination creates dreams of new and original possibilities not yet existing in the world.

Seeing the Big Picture

Children with ADHD are excellent at getting the big picture, in and out of the classroom. Students with ADHD may miss the little details, but they are masters at understanding the importance and meaning of material. For example, children with ADHD may be struck with wonder and awe at the miraculous workings of nature as they learn about photosynthesis and how plants take in sunlight to grow. They may wonder what happens in cloud-covered regions of the world and start to generate ideas for how to get sunlight to plants on cloudy days. As this example illustrates, children with ADHD are often deeply engaged in material in creative and novel ways. They may not remember any of the details about the roles of oxygen and carbon dioxide in the process of photosynthesis, but they are very curious and interested and typically try to create solutions to problems in creative ways.

Typical modes of assessment in the academic world involve being able to repeat small details of abstract processes. This is the most difficult way of learning for children with ADHD. There are few courses of study in the educational system that reward the startling gifts your child has to offer. The good news is that if your child can emerge unscathed from his education, he can find his niche in the real world that will reward him highly for his ardent curiosity, creativity, and ability to solve problems in innovative ways.

The Energy of Impulse

To think daringly original thoughts and to create new ideas or perspectives requires impulsiveness. *Impulsiveness* is the urge to do things or think things that are new and daring, that fall outside the boring grind of the everyday humdrum. Impulsiveness is the urge to forge ahead into new areas of thought and includes a tendency to be bored with whatever everyone else is doing or thinking. It is a necessary ingredient for forging new ground in any area of study or thought.

Distractibility is the tendency to shift one's attention to other arenas. It is the opposite of a horse with blinders plodding along carefully in the path determined by his master. In contrast, people who are distractable will pay attention to thoughts, feelings, or events in the environment that seem to call out to them. They cannot focus because they are enchanted with other aspects of their experience. This is also an essential aspect of creativity, which often manifests in the mixing together of ideas from different domains that seem separate or irrelevant to each other. In Thom Hartmann's book *Attention Deficit Disorder: A Different Perception* (1997), he describes how Thomas Alva Edison, who invented the lightbulb and about a thousand other things, was characterized by an easy distractability. He was known to have forty different inventions in progress at one time. He would work on one until he got bored with it and move on to another one as inspiration hit. Another word for distractibility is "flexibility," and it can be put to use in groundbreaking innovation and productivity.

The open-minded, distractable spaciness of your child is much like the "beginner's mind" that students of Zen Buddhism purposefully try to cultivate. Your child's state of consciousness is, to some people, a highly sought after state of mind, achieved only after years of training. The beginner's mind of Zen Buddhism is so sought after because it allows one to perceive life anew in each moment with freshness and excitement. It lends itself to creativity because rather than imposing outworn modes of understanding on the world, the beginner's mind looks at the world in new and fresh ways. It is a shame that our culture has imposed such a negative stigma on this state of mind that in some disciplines is highly valued.

NATURALLY CREATIVE

Your child is truly gifted to have been given the natural ability to engage in reverie or imaginative thought, to be bold and daring in wanting to bring his imagination into the world, and to be sensitive to inspiration from his thoughts, emotions, or the outside world. In spite of these gifts, he may struggle in school. This is because, in the early years, educational systems focus on a "regurgitation" model. Children are expected to focus attentively, take in material presented in a rigid format, and "regurgitate" it back to the teacher to prove they were listening attentively. This style of learning is contrary to the great gifts your child has been given.

However, it's almost impossible to teach or train people to be creative—a gift with which your child is naturally endowed. It is much easier to train someone who is creative to be disciplined than it is to teach someone who is focused and disciplined to be creative. Your child has the potential for excellence if he can learn to apply discipline to paying attention to details and following through in translating his imaginative flights into completed projects.

In this chapter, you'll do an exercise to experiment with how impulsiveness can lead to creativity. Then you and your child will have the opportunity to reframe and understand his behavior as creative rather than disordered. You will also work on balancing creativity with respect for others.

EXERCISE: DISCIPLINED DAYDREAMING

In order for you to gain some empathy for your child's natural gifts and the potential rewards of spaciness and impulsivity, this exercise will guide you to experiment with purposefully adopting these traits. You will want to get your notebook and a pen handy for recording the impact of these experiments. This exercise also includes prescribing a specified daydreaming session for your child. By setting aside a specified time for daydreaming, you show your support for this aspect of his personality while suggesting that if he can limit his daydreaming to this time, he may get more out of his school time.

Our culture values hard work and achievement above all else. But what happens to the inner voices calling you or your child to goof off, to lie around all day, or to play? In our culture, lounging seems almost criminal. With all the demands for chronic self-improvement, who has time for sitting around and spacing out? What other people call laziness is central to creativity and the discovery and appreciation of life. Genius requires fortuitous insight, imagination, daring originality, and intuition. These are cultivated through getting lost in corners of one's own mind—through play and goofing off.

Opportunities often come from distractions from the well-meaning grind. By staying focused, you may miss the genius-making inspiration. With only rational logic and your nose to the grindstone, you can only climb higher and higher, never gaining the vision that allows you to see where the ladder leads. Alternatively, by spending all of your free time watching TV or playing video games, you are just passively consuming the creative output of other people rather than actively exploring your own inner world. The exercises in this chapter ask you to experiment with indulging your own need to goof off and space out. Remember, this is just an experiment. You may not be able to find the time to allot one half hour a week for the rest of your life, but for one week you should make every effort to cancel unnecessary appointments or commitments and give yourself this opportunity to experience daydreaming.

1. For one week, each day spend one half hour daydreaming. Do not try to solve a specific problem. Do not try to concentrate on one topic. Just let your mind wander wherever it wants to go. Allow yourself to escape if that is what you feel like doing. Purposely bracket this time off, allowing your mind to take whatever paths it wants to take. Invite in fantasies and daydreams.

2. At the end of the week, write in your journal how this experience impacted you. Where did your mind wander during these times? As a parent, your life is filled with enormous responsibilities and concerns that require focus, discipline, and fortitude. What did this period of reverie feel like for you?

3. Experiment with prescribing your child one half hour a day to daydream. Tell him that daydreaming is a wonderful use of imagination that promotes creativity, and so he should do it purposefully for one half hour a day. Invite him to spend the same specified time daydreaming that you are, but make sure you each do it alone.

4. Tell him that when he is tempted to daydream in school, he should remind himself to save it for the special daydreaming time that you have set aside. Tell him that if he thinks of something important he wants to daydream about during school, he can write it down in his notebook and remember to come back to it during his scheduled daydreaming time. If you join him for one week in this experiment, you can spend some time after the daydreaming session to talk about how it felt and what sorts of things you and he spent your time thinking about. You will want to emphasize how you value being spacey and getting lost in imagination.

FEELING GOOD ABOUT FREEING UP TIME

You may feel tempted to not do the preceding exercise and the next one because you feel that there is no way to make time for these experiments. These are experiments in escaping, daydreaming, and allowing yourself and your child a break from rational problem solving and effortful striving. If you find you cannot possibly make the time for these exercises, you may want to review your commitments and see if they are in line with your own values.

For example, are you running your children to multiple commitments each week thinking that each child needs to be involved in a sports activity, an artistic endeavor, and a social event? If so, you might want to give yourself permission to allow your children only one organized activity a week. You may feel guilty, like you are not being a good enough parent or that your kids will not be able to keep up with the other kids who get to be involved in more organized activities. However, children need unstructured time alone and with their parents and siblings. The symptoms of ADHD may be a desperate attempt to give their minds the unstructured time they need to explore. Giving your child this quiet time does him a tremendous service.

Your child needs time away from structured activities for another reason. Many structured activities have an implicit or explicit performance expectation. If your child is in sports, he may feel he has to be good at it or that he is being evaluated and compared to other children. In music disciplines, there is often a sense that children have to achieve mastery of the skills. Most organized activities emphasize some form of achievement. If your child is doing poorly in school, these kinds of activities may be a wonderful outlet for him to receive praise in another area. But they also can become just another setting in which he has to prove himself. The more different activities he is engaged in, the more diffuse and intense the pressure to perform and achieve. This pressure can take its toll on anyone—especially a young child. And it can negatively impact a child diagnosed with ADHD even more intensely. Children with ADHD have a strong need for unstructured time. This is not to say that they should not participate in any extracurricular activities—just that they need fewer. A good place to start would be to set the guideline that each child in your family gets to participate in one activity per week. If the soccer season lasts for four months, then that is all that they can do during that time. They will have to wait for the season to end to join the scout group. Try this as an experiment and see how you, your spouse, and your children respond.

It is important to remember that your child is different from the average child. One of his differences is that he is creative. Creativity requires free time to explore, to play, and to pretend. If much of your child's time is being shaped by structured activities, your child will be restless and disruptive. He needs and prefers the time to explore and create his own structure. Whatever organized activity he's participating in usually involves following through on some activities created by other people. Children with ADHD like to create their own lives and activities.

Similarly, parents need their own downtime and personal lives of their own. If you are spending all of your free time running your children to their commitments, you're not taking good care of yourself. Your marriage needs time for you and your spouse to have adult conversation. If you are single, your romantic life needs you to have energy to spend in connecting with other people. You shouldn't feel guilty for taking time away from your children to put into your love life. Parents who are happily in love will find it easier to be better parents. Taking care of children, particularly those diagnosed with ADHD, takes an enormous amount of energy. The energy generated by a fulfilling connection to a romantic partner can be an important resource for you as a parent. If you spend all of your time taking care of your child, you will soon find yourself depleted, and both you and your child will suffer.

EXERCISE: FULFILL YOUR URGES

This exercise will have one component for parents to try and one for the child. The parents will benefit from this exercise by becoming more sensitive to their own impulses, creating a better understanding of their child's impulsiveness. But your loosening up may help your child in another way. Sometimes, the more rigid parents are in controlling their own impulses, the more impulsive their children are. This is similar to the cliché that the pastor's kids will always be the most rebellious. In her book *Awakening Intuition*, Dr. Mona Shultz links ADHD to intuition and the tendency to act out unexpressed impulses in the family. She writes, that "children with ADD often unconsciously act out any turmoil at home. Mom and Dad fight, then try to smooth the matter over. But Junior trips over the carpet and acts it out physically" (1999, 330). While her example relates to unexpressed tensions, it is also true of unexpressed energies, inclinations, and impulses. For example, if you are overly restrained and never allow yourself to give voice to any irreverent comments, you may find your child blurting out inappropriate comments everywhere you go.

1. Find one full day or a half day where you can spend the time following your own urges. During this time if you want to watch TV all day, do that. If you want to go to the woods and walk around and then eat a hot fudge sundae, then let yourself do that. If you want to sleep most of the time, do that. Allow yourself to closely follow your urges. If some of your impulses are not appropriate to act on, let yourself explore mentally. Ask yourself, "What is underlying this urge? Is there some way I can honor it?" For example, maybe you feel an

urge to call a friend and tell him off. Spend some time think-ing what you would really like to communicate with this friend. Think of how you could communicate your needs to this friend in a way that is not explosively angry. Follow through on taking action based on this realization.

2. Write in your journal how this made you feel. What did you do? How did you feel allowing yourself to indulge your own urges and impulses? Did you learn something new about yourself?

3. Use this experience to help you connect with your child for the next part of the exercise.

4. If your child is five to nine, tell him you want to talk to him about the "Urge Monster." If he is older, you can talk more straightforwardly about uncontrollable urges. You can share with him some of your own urges as an example. Tell your child that everyone has an Urge Monster and that it is impor-tant to feed the monster but not to let it control you. Ask your son to talk about some of his urges and then problem solve with him on ways to control the Urge Monster and to feed it without getting into trouble. An example of how this might go follows.

Dad: Remember when I talked to your teacher about how you were disrupting art class by jumping around and telling everyone that you were going to have a baby sister? Sometimes we all get urges to do things like that and we want to stir things up and blurt out what we really feel. Just today, I thought I'd like to tell my boss to just leave me alone. I realized my boss might get mad at me if I told her what I really thought. But sometimes the Urge Monster just needs to be fed a little bit, and it will quiet down. So I called your Mommy on the phone and told her what I really thought. Then I calmed down and could talk to my boss about what I thought was a more reasonable time frame for me to get my work done, and she agreed with me. How could you learn to feed the Urge Monster?

Sandy: I was just so excited about Samantha in Mommy's belly, and I wanted to tell everybody how good I felt about it. There was no way I could stay quiet.

Dad: How could you feed the urge without disrupting the class? Maybe you could draw a picture of the Urge Monster or draw a picture for your sister when she arrives?

Sandy: Yeah, I bet I could tell the monster that I could wait and tell Daddy how I'm so excited for my sister to get here. And I could draw a picture for my new sister to hang in her bedroom.

Dad: That's a great idea. Sometimes just promising yourself that you will tell someone else will help you keep quiet when the teacher wants you to sit still.

The same urges that cause problems can also be seen as creative urges for self-expression. By learning to feed urges through creative expression, your child can learn to both honor his impulses and channel those urges in creative ways. Creativity often is experienced as an urge to create. When all impulses are suppressed, creativity often gets suppressed, too. Being connected to your impulses and urges is important for both you and your child. For your child diagnosed with ADHD, it allows him access to one of his wonderful gifts—creativity. When creativity is combined with discipline, your child has the potential to be a superstar.

REFRAMING SYMPTOMS: FINDING CREATIVITY

Without paying careful attention to your child's inner process, it is easy to miss his creativity in everyday life. While the teacher complains that he is spacing out during her presentation on the structure of our government, your child may be generating possible solutions for eliminating wasteful governmental spending. While your child appears to be trying to get out of going to his music lessons, he may be singing

Broadway show tunes in his mind with perfect tempo and memory for all the words. If a child isn't doing what he's supposed to be doing, we commonly think he is misbehaving. In fact, he may be exploring and expressing his own unique gifts that do not match up with your tight schedules and plans for him.

For example, what adults often think of as goofing off can be one of the most important activities for any child, but particularly a creative child. If your child is diagnosed with ADHD, you may recognize that he does not have the same attention span and focus of other children, but you must also acknowledge his superior creativity that, as a parent, you are entrusted to nourish and nurture. You do not do this by getting him to conform to the demands of traditional ideas of achievement. You nurture his creativity by making allowances for his differences and unstructuring his life accordingly.

Goofing Off Is Not Giving Up

Creativity requires goofing off. Goofing off is play, experimentation, trying out new ideas, and adjusting them to see what fits, what works, and what is more fun. As a parent, you may have observed your child engaging in an activity for a small amount of time and then after some time of practice the child starts to goof off. For example, one parent complained that her daughter asked to take lessons to learn to play the clarinet. She would practice her lessons at home for only fifteen minutes, then she would put her clarinet down and dance wildly, running around the house like a Tasmanian devil. Her mother considered this giving up. But it can also be viewed as another form of creativity or a strategy for discharging all of her excitement about playing music. It might be her boredom with practicing lessons, which contrasts with her desire to add her own daring and impulsive energy to the practice of the clarinet. Goofing off is not giving up. Parents often get frustrated with children, thinking of how much it costs to buy the clarinet and pay for lessons. In reframing this goofing off as a form of creativity, the child's wild energy can be channeled into creative musical abilities.

Music coach and psychologist Dr. Lane Arye has written in his book *Unintentional Music: Releasing Your Deepest Creativity* about how goofing off can feed one's deepest creativity. As an example, he describes one music lesson with a classical guitarist in which the teacher asked a student to amplify a particular hand gesture that was irrelevant to the music being played. The student amplified his gesture until he was making wild bodily movements and screaming with delight. While this might look beside the point, the teacher writes that after the apparent derailment of the music lesson, "I asked him whether he could express this ecstatic wildness in his music. Franz grabbed his guitar and played the same piece as before. But this time he played it with incredible energy. . . . He said, with an irrepressible smile, that he had never thought it was allowable to play like that" (2001, 109). This interaction can be viewed as a model for parents interacting with their children diagnosed with ADHD. As a parent, you can become a detective and search for ways in which your child's apparent "symptoms" represent creativity or could be channeled to enhance your child's creative expression.

On the Importance of Being Confused

In a similar way, confusion can be reframed as an appreciation for the mysterious, as a humility in the face of the complexity of the world. Your child may get into trouble in school for looking or acting confused when called on or when participating in classroom exercises. Their confusion or apparent disorientation may give the impression that they are not paying any attention at all. It may make them look less intelligent and provoke harsh comments from teachers and students alike. However, this sense of confusion can be reframed as reflecting a higher intellectual sophistication in that it can result from an appreciation of the deeper complexity of the topic being discussed.

Confusion is an admission that one does not fully understand the material being covered. Creativity requires that a person acknowledge that there is more to what is being taught than is covered in the simplifications being presented. Therefore, confusion can also be thought to be a necessary component of creativity. Confusion can represent an experience of the mystery of what is being taught. For example, in reflecting on photosynthesis, a child with ADHD might be awed by the order and harmony in the universe that allows for the sun to nurture plant growth, which in turn nurtures the human environment. A child with ADHD might get derailed in the experience of awe and get confused about the detailed aspects of the biology of photosynthesis. Confusion is essential to creativity but gets a bad rap in our culture, which makes a virtue of being sharp and quick at all times.

These cultural demands overlook the value of being slow and uncomprehending. Often, the constructed explanations offered to students by teachers are oversimplifications. In pretending to know it all, students and teachers gloss over the complexity and mystery of the world. Admitting or experiencing not knowing can be a liberating experience. In fact, the struggle to always have the right answer actually prevents a person from learning. If we think we have the answers, we are not open to a deeper understanding or exploring other ways of seeing the world.

EXERCISE: THE CREATIVITY OF EVERYDAY LIFE

In this exercise you will be asked to practice reframing your child's symptoms as manifestations of creativity. You will be asked to search for ways in which what he is doing can be seen as acting or thinking outside the box. In addition, you will be guided to find ways to honor your child's expression rather than suppress it. You will also ask your child to practice becoming aware of his creativity.

1. Start out by becoming aware of a symptom your child demonstrates. A typical complaint about children with a diagnosis of ADHD is that they don't follow directions very well. For example, when Sam was asked to keep quiet in church, he often seemed to become defiant and would burst out with irreverent comments that the whole congregation could hear. A common vicious cycle that gets set in motion is that the parents interpret this behavior as purposefully defiant and rebuke the child with harsh words and threats of dire consequences if he does not keep quiet.

2. Generate possible positive explanations for how this behavior is creative. For example, you might think that maybe your son is trying to make the services more lively. You might commend him for trying to participate or make a contribution to the church services in his own way. Perhaps your son's irreverence reflects a need for the church services to be more down-to-earth and relevant to the concerns of the parishioners.

3. Engage in a discussion with your son, asking him to reflect on his behavior. Listen, keeping in mind your new frame, which is open to considering nonantagonistic understandings of his behavior. For example, you can calmly ask him why he is contributing to the church service in this way when he was asked to keep quiet. Listen attentively to how your son understands his behavior. He may surprise you by saying that he noticed that people laugh when he makes these outbursts, and he wants people to laugh more at church to show how happy they are to be there. He might tell you that maybe people would come more often if they laughed at church. This is a radically different interpretation of his behavior, seeing it as sweet generosity rather than the more common reaction, which is to understand it as defiant and a symptom of the ADHD diagnosis.

4. Give your son praise for his creativity and remark how this is an example of his ability to think and act in ways that are outside the box. You might also commend him on his perception of the problems with the church service and efforts at problem solving. Remember, creativity means that rather than mastering and following what other people are doing, your child is interested in questioning the way things are done and finding ways of doing things differently.

5. You will also want to tell your son that, while you appreciate his creativity and you think he has a lot to offer, he needs to be aware that some people in church might be disturbed by his outbursts and that the behavior isn't respectful to them. You can explain that while his behavior demonstrates his

gifts, he needs to balance his creative expression with respect for other people.

6. Ask him to engage his creativity in devising ways to express his creativity while still being respectful to everyone else. You can spend some time brainstorming together. For example, you might generate the idea that you could suggest to the minister that rather than having a stuffy choir every week, they could have a jazz band play renditions of some of the hymns. Maybe your son could think of jokes that are not offensive to anyone to tell members of the church during the social hour. Maybe he could paint a picture of people laughing in church and give it to the minister.

Having completed this practice of reframing, communicating, and problem solving with your son, you will be well on your way to increasing your connection. By trying to avoid becoming frustrated and assuming the worst about his behavior, you demonstrate an enormous amount of respect for him. You will also find that by listening to his motivations rather than assuming the worst, you really will gain an increased appreciation for his creativity and positive motivations. The example in this exercise demonstrates how a common reaction of frustration and threats was transformed into increased intimacy. As you change your perceptions, you also transform your child's perceptions of himself. As these ideas change, behavior will follow. You are well on your way to transforming your child's problems into strengths!

EXERCISE: FILL IN THE BLANK

One of the easiest ways to generate positive understandings of your child's behavior is to purposely look for them. For the following exercise, you will write the sentence stems on a piece of lined paper (perhaps in your notebook) and ask your child to fill in the blanks. This can be fun for him because it asks him to use his creativity and gives him a chance to show you what he's really thinking.

1. I am most creative when_____

2. I can show others my imagination by _____

3. I am really good at _____

4. My last really good idea was _____

5. The last idea I had about something that needed to be improved was

_____

6. One thing I do differently from everyone else is _____

7. I do this my way because _____

8. I can help others because _____

9. I can make the world a better place because _____

10. The thing I like most about myself is _____

11. Other people like me because _____

12. I wish people would understand that _____

13. I wish I could show people _____

14. I wish my teacher knew _____

15. I wish my parents knew _____

When you have completed these sentences with your child, you can collaborate in translating some of the results into action. For example, in the case where the child thinks that church needs to be more fun, you can take his comments seriously and suggest that you and he talk with the minister. If you agree that church is too dull, maybe you could try another church. Perhaps you could give him a chance to show the family how he would do a church sermon that would be funny. Once your child's impulse is honored or given expression, you can expect his problematic behavioral expression of it to be reduced.

Let Your Child Contribute

Another reason for honoring your child's impulses is that very often he truly does have something to offer. Sometimes children with ADHD are expressing what a lot of other people really think but are too controlled to say. Thom Hartman, an author and advocate for understanding ADHD as a gift, has argued that the ways in which children diagnosed with ADHD disrupt classes is a sign that our educational system needs to change (1997). If your child insists that classes are boring, he may be exactly right.

In writing on teaching music students, Dr. Lane Arye writes "Old-fashioned ideas about music pedagogy are symptomatic of a larger societal pattern. Both rank and privilege are bestowed on those who are older, better educated, professional, successful. A mere child or someone in a lower socioeconomic position is often forced to humble herself, hold herself back, keep her good ideas hidden, and follow those who have more assigned power.... Being deeply democratic would mean giving the student a say in this process, letting her in on the decisions that affect her education.... For if the needs and ideas of students were taken into consideration, then much of the rebellion that is a normal part of education would be seen as creativity and used to further the teaching process" (2001, 132). The educational system could benefit by giving children more opportunities for creativity, less focus on obedience, more opportunities for engaging their full senses rather than just their minds, and more attention to the individual needs and aptitudes of each student. Not only are you honoring your child by reframing his behavior as potentially creative, you are respecting the impulse toward transforming structures that are not working and are in need of change.

Summary

This chapter reframed the ADHD symptoms of distractibility, daydreaming, and impulsiveness as creativity. Children with ADHD are gifted in imagination and original thought. Specific exercises and strategies were recommended for discovering ways in which what the doctors and teachers call symptoms are actually signs of creativity.

CHAPTER 6

Showing the Way: Ecological Consciousness

Children with the diagnosis of ADHD have a preference for learning about the world through hands-on engagement. They like to be immersed in the topics they are learning about. They are often very curious about the natural and organic world, feeling a deep connection to it. This gift for engaged, experiential learning is often overlooked because existing educational systems focus on abstract learning and rote memorization. What looks like a deficit disorder can be viewed as a mismatch between a preferred way of learning and current standards of teaching and assessment of learning.

Not only do children with a diagnosis of ADHD learn through engagement, they have an ardent curiosity about the living, breathing organic world. They often feel connected and attuned to nature and animals. In their connection to the natural world, they may represent a much-needed force in the world to protect the environment that has been destroyed by seeing the natural world as exploitable and expendable.

In chapter 1, we discussed how anything different from normal often means "disorder" for psychologists, psychiatrists, and teachers. However, to argue that different from normal is bad, one has to believe that normal is good and healthy. In contrast, if one looks at the destruction of the environment, it might be argued that this is the predicament that "normal" modes of consciousness have gotten the world into. Your child's difference may be one that is in some ways better than normal in that she is a candidate to become one who guides us toward a healthier relationship with our environment.

WHAT IS ECOLOGICAL CONSCIOUSNESS?

An ecological consciousness is a way of being that respects the natural world, plants, trees, animals, and insects. Individuals with this form of consciousness feel directly related to and engaged with the natural world. Children with an ecological consciousness often are very sensitive to animals and ardently interested and curious about the natural world. These children like to spend time outside doing anything from getting dirty picking worms and insects out of the dirt to simply rambling. Kids like this usually don't want to sit in a class learning about nature—they want to learn in the natural world. Whereas current education systems demand the focused concentration that learning about the world in terms of abstractions requires, children with ADHD may be gifted in what author David Abram calls "sensuous consciousness" (1996).

The Spell of the Sensuous

David Abram writes in his book *The Spell of the Sensuous* about the devastating impact on our ecology of our disengagement from the natural, organic world we live in. He depicts a culture that has become so absorbed in its own intellectualized abstractions, supported by increasingly sophisticated technologies, that it has become numb to the destruction of our environment. Abram refuses to put forth any utopian solutions to the problems he poses, suggesting that such ideas would themselves invite attention away from sensuous surroundings on behalf of a mental idea. According to Abram,

> A genuinely ecological approach does not work to attain a mentally envisioned future, but strives to enter, ever more deeply, into the sensorial present. It strives to become ever more awake to the other lives, the forms of sentience and sensibility that surround us in the open field of the present moment. (1996, 272)

Abram's discourse offers one avenue for understanding the gifts of what our culture calls an attention deficit. The style of consciousness he advocates as necessary to reverse the damage wrought by the dulling of our senses has much in common with what gets called ADHD. For example, when asked what they are paying attention to in class, children with ADHD often remark that they are looking out the window. They are deeply engaged in observing the trees, birds, or any glimpse of wildlife the window opens up for the child. Often these children are caught by what Abram calls "the spell of the sensuous." This term means that the concrete, everyday world is perceived as almost magical, whereas the abstract world of thoughts and books is not compelling. Abram argues that this a positive quality and entails being enchanted by the world of the senses, often linked to organic natural events.

For example, a student named Mike reported that rather than listening to what was going on in class, he would find himself drawn to watching the way the sun reflected off the leaves of the trees outside the class window and how the wind blew through the leaves and the squirrels played among the branches. He found himself asking why leaves are green and how the squirrels lived off of the tree. From an objective standpoint, it looks like a failure to pay attention to the tasks demanded by our society to absorb the learning of the classroom and succeed in school. From Mike's perspective, this apparent disengagement is actually engagement with the small natural landscape available to him through the window of the classroom.

Mike's interest in the tree and its leaves bespeaks a style of consciousness that is different from modern consciousness. In depicting the modern disengagement from the natural world, Abram amplifies this image of a tree:

> Trees rarely, if ever, speak to us; animals no longer approach us as emissaries from alien zones of intelligence. . . . How is it that these phenomena no longer address us, no longer compel our involvement or reciprocate our attention? . . . To freeze the ongoing animation, to block the wild exchange between the senses and the things that engage them, would be tantamount to freezing the body itself, stopping it short in its tracks. . . . If we no longer experience the enveloping earth as expressive and alive, this can only mean that the animating interplay of the senses has been transferred to another medium, another locus of participation. (130-131)

Importantly, Mike's interest in the tree represents not a deficit disorder or a lack of intrinsic curiosity but an attunement with whatever contact with the natural world he can make in a confined classroom environment. His questioning about what was inside the trees and interest in why the leaves were green reflected a very sophisticated curiosity about the world around him, which was quite advanced for his grade level. So, even though Mike underwent much testing and many visits to doctors to explain his failure in grade school, in fact he was interested in questions that would not be addressed until much later. He would have to wait until high school biology classes to learn about the mechanisms of photosynthesis and the greenness of leaves. It may have been that his difficulties in school resulted from his curiosity far outpacing his grade level, in which he was forced to contend with the mechanics of reading and writing rather than his ardent curiosity about the world around him. Unfortunately, by the time he reached high school he had encountered so many failure experiences that the questions that had originally interested him receded in the background, overshadowed by concerns over his chronically negative evaluations in the academic arena.

Abram suggests that the new locus of participation to which modern culture has transferred its attention is the written text. The abstraction and intellectualization of the modern consciousness has led to a participation not in the world surrounding us but rather in the books and texts that tell us about the world we live in. In depicting the modern evolution of consciousness, from which ADHD is a deviation, Abram writes, "it is only when a culture shifts its participation to these printed letters that the stones fall silent. Only as our senses transfer their animating magic to the written word do the trees become mute, the other animals dumb" (131). Note that for Mike, the trees and animals were alive; it was the book that was dead. Books did not speak as did the organic world outside of the classroom. To Abram, Mike's attention to the spell of the sensuous would not be seen as regressive, but in fact could show a way of being in the world that would facilitate an ecological mind frame. In Abram's words, "it is only at the scale of our direct, sensory interactions with the land around us that we can appropriately notice and respond to the immediate needs of the living world" (268).

To the extent that an attention deficit represents an increased sensitivity to the wider community of nature, this style of consciousness is one that needs to be cultivated to preserve our environment rather than dulled through medication. After all, it is the dulled modern style of consciousness that has led to the growing ecological crisis our culture faces. Abram links the imperviousness to the spell of the sensuous with the destruction of our ecosystems and the extinction of many species.

A TALE OF TWO STUDENTS

While ADHD can be seen to represent a form of sensuous consciousness with many gifts to offer, you are familiar with how this gift can play out negatively in the classroom. Below are brief characterizations of two students, one with "normal" modes of paying attention (Sam) and the second with an ecologically engaged consciousness (John).

> Sam is sitting quietly in science class. He is focused intently on what the teacher is saying about the structure of flowers. Some of the information is familiar from Sam's reading in the textbook. Sam wants to pay careful attention to what the teacher says because he knows there will be a quiz soon on the anatomy of a flower. He wants to do well on the quiz.

> John is having a hard time staying in his seat. The teacher is droning on and on about something, but John is mesmerized by the scene from his classroom window. He's watching the rain fall on the plants and trees near the fence across the street. John wonders if the plants and trees drink the water and why they don't get soggy. He wonders if all the insects get washed off the plants and trees and if they need to drink water from the rain. John hasn't kept up with his reading because the book seemed really boring. When he tried to do his homework the night before, he was too busy watching the neighbor's dog chase squirrels to focus on the text.

As you can see from these two vignettes, both students are paying attention—just to different things. One student pays attention to books, teachers and the importance of getting good grades. Sam remembers that there will be a quiz on the material and this motivates him to pay attention. The other student pays attention to trees, leaves, and animals. John shows ardent curiosity in understanding the world around him. Sam will likely succeed in school. John will probably do poorly. Both are curious and smart. However, John's failure in school will likely lead him to believe that he's not smart. He may begin to believe that he just doesn't measure up and will never succeed, so he'll give up trying in school. John may begin to think there must be something wrong with him, wondering, "Why do I always fail?"

It may that John is being failed by the school system. There are many learning strategies that might tap into John's gift of engagement with the sensual world. For example, if rather than being assigned reading, John was assigned the task of exploring a garden, observing the flowers, and bringing a flower to class, he might then be interested in paying attention to what is going on in the classroom. Because children with ADHD learn through their senses, anchoring lessons firmly in the sensual world of experience will help them to maintain an interest in tracking what is happening in the classroom.

For example, if your daughter has been assigned to find a flower and enters the classroom after exploration and observation, she will likely have used her ardent curiosity and creativity to have generated many questions about the flower. Her questions will serve as a hook to keep her interest in the classroom discussion and activities. As a parent, you can engage your child's interest by encouraging these interests rather than dismissing them as distractions. For example, rather than forcing your child to sit down before dinner and read quietly, you can find out what the material to be covered is and allow for some time to observe or explore in ways related to lesson plans. If you cannot find a way to connect the material with sensual learning, you might offer an opportunity for nature exploration around the neighborhood to help your child prepare for book learning.

A recent study by researchers Faber-Taylor and colleagues found that the symptoms of ADHD were relieved by time spent in nature (2001). The study found that children were more able to concentrate, complete tasks, and follow directions after spending play time in natural, especially green, settings. Activities such as camping, fishing, or playing soccer outside were examples of time spent in natural settings. The authors suggested that these findings cannot be explained just by the subjects being active. For example, playing basketball in paved surroundings did not result in the improvements in concentration that even passive activities in green settings did. Also, the results were not just because children engaged in preferred activities and so were willing to settle down. The researchers found that, while children's preferred activities were watching TV or playing video games, these activities did not improve symptoms as playing in nature did.

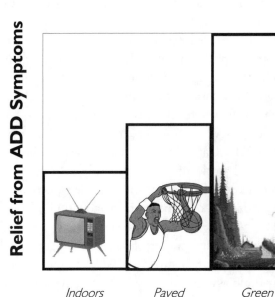

ADD symptoms in children are relieved after spending time in nature. The greener the setting, the more the relief.

Relief from ADD Symptoms

Indoors   *Paved Outdoors*   *Green Outdoors*

The authors explain their findings by suggesting that being in nature facilitates a state of involuntary attention that is effortless and provides a rest from directed attention. *Directed attention* is the capacity to focus narrowly. The authors argue that the use of directed attention is like a muscle and gets fatigued. The involuntary attention that is promoted by activity in nature provides a rest, allowing the child to exert directed attention after having been in nature.

Another explanation that supplements the authors' findings is that children with ADHD have a particular attunement to nature and that feeding this need helps them to settle down. In some ways, children with this diagnosis need to be connected to nature and are unsettled until this need is met.

Further research support for the power of nature was found for at-risk inner-city girls. One study found that the greener the view from a girl's home (meaning the more nature was visible from a window), the more that girl was able to concentrate, inhibit impulses, and delay gratification (Faber-Taylor et al. 2002). While this study found this effect only for girls in this sample, the results suggest that when children who have difficulty concentrating stare out windows in the classroom, they may be attempting to heal themselves. This has implications for how students staring out windows are treated, in the sense that this behavior is usually punished or pointed to as evidence of not trying at all. In fact, it may be providing the rest the child needs in order to proceed.

ENCOURAGING YOUR CHILD'S ATTUNEMENT TO NATURE

Given that your child's way of being in the world and easy connection to nature can be understood as a gift, it may be to her benefit to encourage the development of this talent. It's possible that honoring this gift outside the classroom will allow your child to pay attention inside the classroom. There are many strategies you can use to honor your child's gift and shape her behavior to achieve greater success in school. For one, you never want to punish your child by taking away her time in nature. Because this time is what she needs to help her concentrate, you would put her in a bind if you take away her time in nature as a punishment for not following directions or doing homework. Another implication is that it is not effective to use time in nature as a reward. For example, it is more helpful to have time in nature precede schoolwork than to say that if your daughter completes her homework, then she can play outdoors. She may very well need her time in nature to facilitate doing her homework.

Because attunement to nature increases your child's ability to focus, it is a better strategy to allow her play time in nature before study time. The main idea here is that you want to work with your child's natural gifts rather than working against them. By realizing that your child feels a special connection to nature and by knowing that this connection is healing for her, you can use play time in nature as a preparation to help her focus, concentrate, and follow through on directions. You may want to create a schedule for your child that involves nature time before asking her to engage in homework or household chores.

You will also want to boost your child's self-esteem by honoring this gift. You can tell her directly that you understand and value the importance of her connection to animals, trees, and the organic living world. You can also tell her that her engagement with nature is a great gift to offer the world. You can talk about the environmental problems in the world and how this results from thinking that nature is not important compared to human wants and needs. You can tell her how her direct connection to nature represents a different style of being in the world that serves to balance the disregard that can be seen in the normal state of mind. You can also tell her that what the doctors call ADHD is this different state of mind, and that it is different from normal, but different in this good way.

Project-Based Learning Strategies

Another strategy for using your child's engagement with the natural world is to develop project-based learning exercises for her. This means that, for example, in science classes you try to engage her senses with field trips and exploration of the world. You will want to help your child connect with the world outside the classroom while also advocating for project-based learning strategies to your child's teachers.

This type of learning exercise asks children to actually do things rather than just reading about them. Children with a diagnosis of ADHD have a hard time with processing abstractions or rational, linear representations of the world. However, they can be very effective in solving real-world problems and learning through engagement with the world. As a parent, you can engage your child's interest by introducing her to a project or experience that helps to illuminate the topic she's studying in class. The following exercise is an example that is more relevant to science or literature classes. But if you can increase your child's motivation in one topic of interest, and she can demonstrate success in one subject, her sense of self-esteem and efficacy will increase, boosting her motivation for other subjects. As she learns that she is capable of succeeding, her enthusiasm will be enhanced and she'll believe that with effort, she can succeed.

EXERCISE: CREATING YOUR OWN FIELD TRIPS

1. Choose a subject area or topic from school that lends itself to spending time in nature. Usually this will be a science.

Sometimes you can engage your child's interest in literature by connecting some of the natural elements of the story to real-world explorations. As an example, if the story takes place near a lake, you can plan a trip to a lake or pond to motivate her to engage with the reading material.

2. Plan and develop a trip or project that will engage your child's senses and is related to your chosen subject. For instance, if your child is learning about animals, plan a trip to the zoo. If she's learning about trees, plan a trip to a forest and ask her to pick out some leaves.

3. Provide praise for your child's energy and ability to follow directions as she participates in the project or exploration. In this way you are validating that she does have the skills to follow directions, to focus her energy, and to learn new things. You can also validate her creativity and curiosity. When your child's full senses are engaged in learning, her gifts will be evident as she shows a lot of energy, curiosity, and creativity in exploring the world. Reflect back to your child your appreciation of these gifts.

4. Connect these gifts back to book learning and school. Once you have engaged her curiosity, have her think about all of the questions about the topic area that are bound to arise. Tell her that the books she has for school and her teacher can help her find answers to these questions. So for example, after a trip to a nearby forest to collect leaves, you can direct her to some readings that talk about the structures and function of leaves. In this way you can channel your child's energy and enthusiasm into finding answers through books and school. This will increase her motivation to participate in the classroom.

Another strategy for connecting book learning and sensual learning is to allow your child to learn in nature. If you can find a nearby park that has picnic tables, maybe you can allow her to study or read for some amount of time at the park. Again, this strategy allows you to go with the flow rather than resist your child's natural inclination to be in nature.

Advocate for Project-Based Learning in School

A personal testimony of the value of project-based learning for students with ADHD can be found in the book *Learning Outside the Lines*, written by two students with ADHD who made it through an Ivy League school (Mooney and Cole 2000). These students describe their personal struggle with school and how they overcame their obstacles to succeed in a university setting. They advocate for the use of project-based learning as one way of navigating through the educational system. These authors write about how simple changes in the learning environment can make or break academic success: "Only as time went on did simple interventions like the ability to get up out of our seats, the use of a spell checker, and progressive ideas like project-based learning and other modifications to the learning environment allow the pathology to slip into irrelevance and enable us to be successful" (65).

As a parent, you can become an advocate for having these changes made for your child. These same authors talk about having teachers who emphasized spelling and tormented them with bad grades and public humiliation because they couldn't spell. The authors learned to hate school and associate it with personal failure. One of the authors tells a dramatic story about how one teacher, understanding the child's differences, did not penalize the student for spelling or emphasize it. This teacher allowed the student to use a spell-checker and one of the main struggles of elementary school was ended. This teacher looked for and saw the strengths of the student and emphasized those. These simple changes in the environment can have powerful effects on your child's success and attitude toward school.

If even small changes, like permission to use a spell-checker, can make such dramatic changes, you can imagine the benefits of larger changes, such as incorporating project-based learning into your child's coursework. As an advocate for your child, you can meet with each teacher and make them aware of your child's diagnosis and the importance of project-based learning as an adjunct to regular classroom learning. You can also advocate that your child's grades be based on projects rather than quizzes or tests.

Each time you advocate for changes in your child's instruction, you should let your child know what you're doing and why you are doing it. In this way, your child will grow to feel that you are on her side and not an antagonist. The power of her sense of being supported cannot be overstated. As your child feels that you are advocating for her interests, her motivation to do well in school and to work hard will be increased. In addition, by advocating for her differences, you are communicating to her that her differences are not deficits. You are also recognizing that she has strengths. Your daughter will internalize the self-esteem that is conveyed by your advocating for her to her teacher and taking action to change the environment rather than just trying to change her. As you place, in part, some of the blame for her failures on the school environment, you can reverse the self-blame and self-defeating thoughts that plague your child.

An example of what you might say to a teacher follows:

Mr. Welch, I wanted to speak to you about how you can best facilitate my daughter's learning in your class. I have come to see that Janet has a different style of learning.
She shows a special engagement with nature and the organic living world and learns best when she is doing and touching and able to get her hands on whatever is being studied. She struggles with details and abstractions, but is highly curious. I have found that I can increase her motivation for book learning if I tie it to some project or exploration of the organic world. For example, I see you have a quiz planned on labeling the parts of a flower. If you can involve the class in looking for real flowers or bring in real flowers and ask them to explore, touch, and develop questions about the flowers, it would be a great help to Janet. I'm not trying to tell you how to teach your class, but I know you have a commitment to reaching each child and engaging their interest in science. This is one way that really works with my daughter.

In addition to advocating for project-based learning, you might also want to talk to teachers about strategies of punishment that are likely to fail for your child. It's common for teachers to punish ADHD students for goofing off in class by taking away their recess time. You might want to advocate for your child that recess and time out in nature help her to concentrate and settle down. Once the teacher takes this away, her behavior is likely to get worse, not get better. Sometimes this form of handling behavior leads to a vicious cycle. Your child has difficulty sitting still in class and the teacher says that if she cannot sit in her seat, she'll miss recess. Your child gets out of her seat and misses recess, which is her time to connect with nature. In subsequent classes, her behavior gets worse and more forms of behavioral control and punishment follow, which humiliate your child. All of this makes her feel more negative toward school and more and more out of control of her own behavior.

The ecological consciousness of children with ADHD suggests a radical intervention for these children. Rather than taking away their recess time, they need more time for breaks. You might also make this radical suggestion to your child's teacher. It may be that instead of time-outs or trips to the principal's office after bad behavior, the school could implement preventative steps by giving your child small breaks outside in nature before classes.

Schools and teachers regularly make allowances for children with ADHD. The problem is these allowances are usually stigmatizing. Students may be taken out of class to go to reading remediation or other interventions that other students make fun of. These interventions are almost always humiliating and difficult for your child to tolerate. It seems worth advocating for your child's teachers and schools to allow for small nature breaks in place of other forms of remedial intervention.

Similarly, small allowances in the classroom can prevent major outbursts. Simple behavioral interventions like permitting a child to get out of her seat on occasion can go a long way toward making school more tolerable for your child. As a parent, you can ask for behavioral interventions that are not punishing or humiliating for your child. These minor allowances can prevent major interruptions in the classroom.

Jonathan Mooney and David Cole, the authors of *Learning Outside the Lines* say:

> For sure we had certain weaknesses (spelling, attention span), but we also had enormous strengths for learning outside the lines that were obvious when we were children, but went underutilized and were never valued by our schools. Not only were we labeled as diseased, but we also lost the opportunity to be educated in the most appropriate way for our individual minds. We lost our opportunity to enjoy elementary school; instead, learning became a struggle. Trapped as children by a narrow understanding of what it means to learn, we lost our passion for learning and our passion for school, which we had to fight to regain later in our lives. We also lost the opportunity to develop the intuitive, emotional, and creative parts of our minds. These were identified as irrelevant, as learning became about memorization and sequential thinking, and not about creative, intuitive ideas. (2000, 70)

These words may serve as an inspiration for you to take a proactive role in asking for changes in your child's learning environment. It's important to remember that your child's school is already changing the environment to accommodate your child. Your child may be subjected to frequent time-outs, trips to the principal's office, sitting in the hallway during recess, and time out from the regular schedule for remedial interventions and to take medications. As an advocate, you're simply asking for changes in the environment that will prevent problems by enhancing your child's passion for learning. Your child's behavior is currently being managed by the environment, but likely in a negative way. Instead of punishment, ask for prevention.

MATCHING ENVIRONMENTS AND EXPECTATIONS TO YOUR CHILD

Given the power of the environment to impact your child's behavior, you may want to begin to think about how to create environments that are a good match for your child's differences and gifts. You don't have to lower your expectations for your child's level of achievement, but you should be sensitive to which directions are most likely to suit your child's natural abilities. An enormous amount of what looks like psychopathology can actually be a terrible match between a person's natural gifts and their environment. For example, imagine how depressed and anxious a creative, artistic person would be as a computer programmer in a Fortune 500 company. In some way, your child is stuck in a situation like this. Her gifts are a bad fit for the way in which most schools structure learning environments.

As a parent, you may want to build on your child's interests that won't be met in the classroom. Very early, you can begin to take seriously your child's interests in the natural world or other areas of special interest and begin providing guidance for how she might make a career out of these interests. As a general rule for activities and career directions, try to encourage your child in pursuits that build on existing strengths rather than trying to fill in for weaknesses.

While it may seem that it is way too early for you to think about career choices for your child, the expectations you have now deeply affect her perceptions of what is and is not an acceptable direction to move in. Some children close off interests at a very early age because parents convey that these interests aren't serious enough. It is important to remember that any specialized interest your child expresses can be thought of as fuel for driving her interest in the academic arena. If she has an almost obsessive interest in dinosaurs, you can use that interest to get her interested in reading books on dinosaurs or taking trips to natural history museums. If your child has an avid interest in sports, you can use that to develop her interest in math as she tries memorizing stats on favorite players and learning what the various numbers mean.

Sometimes parents make the mistake of suppressing interests that don't fit in with their expectations for their child. A child who loves sports may later develop an interest in how to create a strong and healthy body to excel in sports, which may then transform into an interest in medicine. A child who loves to play with animals may develop knowledge and curiosity that leads her to a career as a veterinarian. Children who love listening to music may be motivated to learn to read it, which can facilitate the learning of math skills.

In this way, your child's natural attunement to nature can be encouraged and can suggest directions for vocational interests later in life. Children with ADHD can grow up to be conservationists, marine biologists, or county employees for managing and protecting water resources. While book learning is a struggle for individuals diagnosed with ADHD, if they achieve the discipline to make their way through higher education, they can make excellent doctors or veterinarians. While the demanding rigors of a premed program and medical school are an obstacle, many ADHD students are capable of sticking it through. If they do, their sensuous consciousness serves them well as medical doctors. They can have an intuitive connection with organic, living anatomy.

The main theme is that while you do not need to do career counseling for your young child, you should not let your expectations deter your child from pursuing any interest that she is passionate about. Not only can her natural curiosity be channeled to fuel academic skills, the interest itself can become a content area that will serve her later in life.

On a much broader scale, your child's interest in nature has the potential to serve the world and offer a balance to current mind-sets that devalue the environment as exploitable for commercial ends. Your child's sensitivity may lead her to a satisfying career in conservation or preservation of the natural world.

Summary

This chapter reviewed the way in which symptoms of ADHD can be seen as a form of ecological consciousness or engagement with the natural world. Rather than being a deficit or disorder, ADHD may represent a surplus of sensuous attunement with plants, trees, and animals.

CHAPTER 7

Interpersonal Intuition

A DIFFERENT TAKE ON RELATING
TO OTHERS

One of the most painful aspects for parents of children diagnosed with ADHD to endure is to observe their child experience peer rejection. Children with ADHD are often charged with inappropriate boundaries and impulsive behavior that alienates their peers and teachers. This chapter will help you see your child's interpersonal style as a precocious but sometimes irreverent gift for understanding human interactions.

The following account illustrates how you, too, can transform your vision of the interpersonal style of ADHD. A therapist-in-training, Amy Williams, reported feeling anxious about her responsibilities as coleader of a group therapy treatment for adolescent girls. As a new therapist, her anxiety was predictable as she assumed this new role. As the group developed, her anxiety turned to dismay as she realized that one of the group members who had been diagnosed with ADHD was unmanageable. This member was loud and obnoxious and disrupted the group at every turn. Amy felt like she was losing control of the group and worked hard to keep it on track. After weeks of group therapy that seemed out of control because of the disruption caused by this one member, Amy mentally gave up. She walked into the next group meeting with the realization that she could not manage this group, and she would just have to stick it out. She accepted defeat and, in so doing, banished her anxiety. No longer was she intent on making the group work perfectly, or doubting herself if she couldn't control its course.

Amy reported a remarkable transformation. The very day she conquered her anxiety, the group process transformed. The one member who had been so disruptive suddenly was the model group client. The group therapy proceeded, and for the first time the process facilitated healing for all members.

In Amy's account of this remarkable transformation, she realized that the client with ADHD had been acting out Amy's anxiety about managing the group and her new role. And, as the client continued disrupting the group, Amy's anxiety escalated. A vicious cycle was set in motion as the client's behavior grew worse and Amy became more anxious. As soon as Amy dissipated her own anxiety by giving up, the vicious cycle was stopped and the client's behavior was no longer disruptive or disturbed. Amy remarked that her first impressions of this client were that she was pretty superficial and incapable of connecting to others. After realizing the startling connection between her own emotional state and this client's behavior, Amy saw that this client was more connected to her than any other client was. In fact, this client was so attuned to Amy's emotional state that she acted it out. This transformation from seeing the client as superficial and obnoxious to highly sensitive, attuned, and connected to her will serve as a template for understanding the interpersonal gifts of ADHD.

FREE-FLOATING AWARENESS

This intuitive ability that children diagnosed with ADHD have bears a striking resemblance to the same gifts that therapists try to cultivate to understand their clients.

Once recognized, the gift can be transformed into an ability to connect deeply with others. ADHD may be likened to the free-floating awareness advocated by psychoanalysts as a way of picking up what the clients may be feeling. This style of awareness may allow the individual with ADHD to be more attuned to other people in spite of their inability to pay close attention to the words being said. This inability to listen carefully to others, a common symptom of ADHD, might be akin to what Freud called "evenly-hovering attention," which "simply consists in making no effort to concentrate the attention on anything in particular. . . . [O]ne proceeds aimlessly, and allows oneself to be overtaken by any surprises, always presenting to them an open mind, free from any expectations" (1963, 118-120). Freud thought that this form of attention was a talent necessary for listening with the "third ear" or for developing what might be called interpersonal intuition. One of the gifts of children diagnosed with ADHD can be thought of as this talent to discern what's not being said, the ability to read the emotions of others.

One college student with ADHD reported that she felt one of the reasons she had a hard time listening to others was because she so often recognized that what a person was saying was in contradiction to what was really going on with them. She found herself paying close attention to a person's nonverbal cues, facial expressions, and gestures and felt able to read what was really going on with the individual. Again, while it may have seemed like she was not paying attention at all, often she was very present and aware of the other person but in ways that aren't typical. This may be understood as an ability rather than a deficit. By this student's account, her inability to focus allows her to understand other people more deeply because she isn't guided simply by words. ADHD may be seen as an intuitive intelligence that picks up the present state of individuals that they may not want to convey.

The problem for a child with ADHD is that he cannot stop his interpersonal intuition and sensitivity to others' emotions from flooding his experience. Because a child cannot process intense emotions, he will often resort to acting out the emotions of others in disruptive behavior. The exercises in this chapter will help your child channel his gift in productive ways.

EMOTIONAL CONTAGION

You can help your child understand his gift by describing it to him as "emotional contagion." Like a cold or a flu, other people's emotions can be caught, and your child easily catches them. This doesn't mean he's disabled or disordered, because it allows him to understand others in a different and deeper way.

The steps to transform this sensitivity into a gift are first, to help your child become aware of the emotion he feels; second, help him figure out whose emotions he is being sensitive to; and finally, help him communicate his sensitivity to the person. There are also some strategies for helping your child protect himself from being so sensitive. The following exercises will help your child manage his emotional sensitivity to others.

EXERCISE: WHOSE FEELING IS THIS ANYWAY?

Ask your child to remember an example of a behavior of which he felt out of control and which he couldn't explain at the time. As he tells you about the example, ask him who was most disrupted by the behavior or was the target of the behavior. Get as many concrete details as possible about the situation. It may be useful to start with an example that involves you, because then you can validate his feelings or explore them in greater depth.

When you have a very vivid picture in your mind of what happened, ask your child to take a few deep breaths and settle down. After he takes a few breaths, ask him to focus on what he was feeling at the time of the disruptive incident. You can help him by asking the following questions:

- Where do you feel it in your body?

- How big is the feeling?

- What color is the feeling?

- Is it hot or cold?

- Is it sharp or dull?

- Is it hard or soft?

- Does it make you more tired or give you more energy?

- What shape is it?

- Is it heavy or light?

- Is it strong or weak?

- Is it mad?

- Is it sad?

- Is it afraid?

- Is it excited?

- Is it happy?

- Is it upset?

- Is it disgusted?

- Is it surprised?

- What does it look like?

- Does it move?

- What name would you give it?

As you go through these questions, help your child get a strong impression of the emotion and help him define it or clarify the feeling.

Once your child has described the feeling, tell him that sometimes he may catch feelings from other people. He may start feeling things that aren't really his feelings. Then you might ask him to speculate whose feeling it might have been in that situation. If the feeling involves a reaction to you, he might say, "I was just running around when you came to school to talk to the teacher. I didn't know why I couldn't stop, but I was afraid." You might want to explore if there was a way in which you were afraid and he was sensitive to it. You might say, "You are very sensitive to have picked up on that feeling, because I was nervous talking to your teacher. I was afraid he would think I was a bad mom, and I was afraid I would get mad at him for being impatient with you." In this way you may be able to validate his feelings as mirroring your own. If the feelings aren't related to yours, you can still help him practice slowing down to feel what it is, describing it in as much sensory detail as possible, and putting a name on it.

Because children often act out feelings rather than feel them, helping your child slow down and feel, name, and describe what's going on inside of him will help manage his behavior. Once he is aware of his feelings, he won't act them out. Once he gains this awareness, he can talk about and can use his gift to increase intimacy with others.

You can show your child how he can use his feeling to communicate a sense of connection with others. In the example above, you might suggest he ask you, "Are you afraid, Mommy?" As he begins translating his inner experience into a gift for connecting with others, people will respond differently to him. The very same emotions that previously disrupted his behavior can now be channeled into forging connections with others.

After practicing this process with you, invite him to practice applying it at school with his peers. You can role-play an interaction with a friend. For example, play a game of pretend. Ask your child to imagine that you are his cousin Kate. Describe a real-life example that ended in disruption. As an example, remind your child of the time Kate's little brother started calling Kate names. While Kate continued to play calmly, your child starting throwing blocks at Kate's little brother. After going through the steps described above, role-play having your child say something to Kate like, "I bet you're mad at your little brother. He's really acting like a pest." Then you can role-play Kate affirming your child, feeling even closer to your son, and continuing to play without disturbance.

EXERCISE: FORCE-FIELD CONTROL

This exercise is an imaginary game that your child can use to help protect himself from being so sensitive to catching other people's emotions. All children are very sensitive and feel the emotions in any setting or situation. Children with a diagnosis of ADHD tend to be even more sensitive and emotional. The intensity of your child's connection to other people's emotions is one of the reasons he is so impulsive and sometimes out of control. Often he feels a lack of control because he is being pushed and pulled by emotions that aren't his own. He may find it difficult to concentrate as he feels the emotions of those in his environment pulling him off track.

In this exercise you will help your child to protect himself from his emotional sensitivity. He will learn to use the feeling of being out of control as a signal that he is tuned in to someone else's emotional state.

1. Ask your child to identify how he knows when he is getting out of control. Ask him to identify the earliest warning signs he can think of. He may describe feelings of being overwhelmed, of feeling pushed, or of feeling like there is a motor in him making him do things. Whatever he uses to describe the feeling, validate the feeling and tell him that this is an important warning sign that he needs to pay close attention to.

2. Ask him to pay attention for one week to what he feels before, during, and after every episode of feeling out of control. For this week, you're not trying to change his behavior, you are just trying to observe it. Every day after school, ask him how school went and if there was an incident where he felt out of control. Ask him to describe in as much detail, using the questions from the first exercise, what that out-of-control feeling was like. Any time you observe him in a state where he loses control, ask him to stop and observe what that feels like.

3. Develop a very detailed sensory description of what being out of control feels like. It may be something like, "I feel like a gush of energy, and I can't stop myself. Sometimes I know I shouldn't do what I'm doing, but I feel like there is a jet engine making me move. I feel it as a stomachache, and usually it feels like a bright red color that's shaking." Have him elaborate on the description as much as possible.

4. Tell your child that he can think of this feeling as a warning signal. It means "Stop!" Ask your child to take one week to pay attention to when he experiences this feeling. Whenever he gets the feeling during the week, he should practice stopping and taking a few breaths.

5. After having completed the earlier steps of monitoring his out-of-control behavior and practicing stopping at the warning signal, spend some time teaching him the following pretend game. Teach your child to use an imaginary force field to provide a buffer between him and other people's emotions. Ask him to imagine that he has control over an invisible force field that can keep out impulses. Let him create this field in his imagination with as much embellishment as possible. For example, he may imagine a pink force field of energy that vibrates and any impulses bounce off as soon as he senses them. He might imagine the field as a yellow bubble that surrounds him and protects him from impulses. Spend some time showing him how he can control this force field. He can make it go up, and he can make it go down. He can make it thicker or thinner. He can make it extend far from him or closer to him. He can make it change color. He can make it stronger or weaker.

6. Tell your child that, for the next week, as soon as he feels his warning sign, he should practice using his force field. At the earliest sign that his warning signal is coming on, he can play this imaginary game.

7. When the week is over, ask your child to describe what happened when he used his force field. If the outcome was good, reinforce how much it helped and encourage him in using it. If the results were not as good as he'd hoped, help him problem solve about how he could use it in a better way. Encourage him to keep practicing this imagination game.

FROM DEFIANT TO SELF-RELIANT

Children who have been diagnosed with ADHD are often perceived as interpersonally defiant or oppositional. It is this quality that most provokes teachers and sets up a negative interaction cycle. The teacher's perception of and reaction to your child will have a powerful impact on his behavior, motivation, and success in school.

Because your child is so interpersonally sensitive, he will feel the teacher's judgment of him and act it out in class, setting up yet another vicious cycle. The way this one works looks something like this: Your child's teacher knows your child has been diagnosed with ADHD, so at the first sign of disruption, she reacts very negatively. Your son picks up on her negative feelings and begins acting them out, causing even more disruption. Then the teacher punishes your child, embarrassing him. Now your son not only feels compelled to act out the teacher's increasingly negative feelings, but he also reacts strongly to being humiliated in class. Rather than being able to identify his feelings as being embarrassed by the teacher, your child is more likely to try to show the teacher he doesn't care by acting out even more. The teacher's negative judgments and punitive behavior can create behavior that is, in fact, defiant—an attempt to defy the teacher's seeming rejection of your child.

Even though this pattern of interaction can set up defiant behavior, often your child's initial behavior is a form of self-reliance that gets interpreted as defiance. The teacher's tendency to interpret self-reliance as defiance is what sets up the initial rejection that leads to the vicious cycle described above. For example, a common disruption is when a child gets out of his seat without asking permission. He may feel confident and not want to bother the teacher.

As mentioned earlier in the book, the teacher's interpretations of your child's behavior can have dramatic effects on your child's attitudes toward education and the course of his motivation and achievement. Recent research has found that teachers may be the force behind the dramatic increases in the diagnosis of ADHD. One study found that teachers are usually the first person to suggest the diagnosis of ADHD (Sax and Kautz 2003). Researchers who surveyed pediatricians, psychiatrists, and family physicians found that in 47 percent of cases of diagnosed ADHD, the teacher was the person who first suggested the diagnosis.

The implication of this finding is that teachers have a great deal of power in the diagnosis and course of ADHD. It emphasizes that, as a parent who has a child diagnosed with ADHD, your efforts to work with the teacher are essential to your child's transformation. It also suggests that if your child's diagnosis was suggested by a teacher, you may want to consider the validity of the diagnosis. Although teachers don't make diagnoses, they usually are asked to fill out rating forms that psychologists and psychiatrists use in assessment. Often teachers are overworked and have too many children in classes with too few resources. They may have little tolerance for having to manage behavior and may find that a diagnosis of ADHD leads to medications that make a child easier to control in the classroom. Teachers often have good intentions for your child, but they have bought into the medical model of ADHD. They often believe that it is a medical disorder rather than a behavioral disorder that can be caused and cured by changing thoughts, behavior, and environments.

Children with ADHD are also often perceived as sensitive and charismatic. Your child's energy and sensitivity can make him fun to be around. However, in tightly controlled classrooms, your child's charisma might again be interpreted as defiance. As a parent, you can become an advocate for your child and help shape teachers' perceptions of your child.

Part of the interpersonal gift of ADHD is that your child can be the class clown or a similar bright light. The problem is that in a classroom that emphasizes conformity and control, your child will be subjected to punishment and humiliation that can lead these gifts to degenerate into defiance.

The emphasis on control in the classroom serves the purpose of managing classes that are too large. Your child's best interests are served by teaching him to think for himself, to learn to trust his inner knowing. Success in the real world depends more on being able to think for yourself than being able to sit still and memorize facts. On a much larger scale, the atrocity of Nazi Germany can, in part, be attributed to a nation that did not permit its citizens to think for themselves. On a smaller scale, you want your child to be able to think for himself as he becomes a teenager and is subject to strong peer pressures. For these reasons, as a parent you want to encourage your child's ability to think for himself. You will also want to advocate to teachers and school administrators that this capacity be appreciated.

There is a cultural element in your child's being labeled as oppositional or defiant. Ours is a culture that values teaching children conformity and compliance over self-reliance. The increasing rates of diagnosis of ADHD may point to a failing in our educational system rather than a medical problem in your child. The terms "oppositional" and "defiant" are relational terms. One can only defy another person; it can only happen in a relationship, not in isolation. Therefore the labels may also be pointing to that which is being defied.

EXERCISE: CATCH YOUR CHILD IN ACTS OF SELF-RELIANCE

In order for you to change your own interactions with your child and to become her advocate in school settings, you will need to practice changing your own interpretations of her behavior. Try the following exercise.

1. For one week, simply monitor your judgments of what you might think of as your child's oppositional behavior. Keep a journal of the behaviors that you felt were defiant, situations in which you wanted something, and she refused or argued with you. Observe these situations, handle them as you usually do, and carefully note your reactions, emotions, and the outcome of the situation. As an example, you might note that "I told Sarah that her friends had to go home because she had to clean up her bedroom before dinner. Sarah got angry and said she was in the middle of putting on a play based on *The Wizard of Oz*, and she wanted to finish. I felt impatient and tired, and I told Sarah that she would not be able to have her friends over next week if she couldn't follow my directions. She started crying and got mad at me. Her friends were obviously uncomfortable, and after they left, Sarah refused to clean her room and didn't talk at all during dinner."

2. For the next week, practice episodes of redefining your child's defiance as self-reliance in the moment. Try to see the situation as her thinking for herself, and consider that she may be right. In many situations, this won't be appropriate. For example, if your child is cursing or hitting, you want to be sure to exert control in the situation. However, if you can find one or two situations in which your child may be right, then change your behavior to reflect your newfound appreciation for your child's self-reliance. As an example, if a situation like the one described above were to happen, you might note, "I told Sarah that her friends had to go home because she had to clean up her bedroom before dinner. Sarah got angry and said she was in the middle of putting on a play, and she wanted to finish. I was curious as to how she knew how to put on a play and told her I wanted to watch for a few minutes. I saw that she was directing her friends in a creative rendition of *The Wizard of Oz,* having each of her friends play a different role. I realized how creative she was being and capable in helping her friends play their part. I commented to her and her friends how creative and talented they were, but reminded Sarah that dinner would be ready in twenty minutes. I told her she could clean her bedroom after dinner, but that she would still have to finish the play in ten minutes so she could say good-bye to her friends and get cleaned up before dinner. Sarah said that was okay, that in ten minutes they could end at a part that made sense."

3. Use your experience of reframing defiance into self-reliance to become an advocate for your child. Make an appointment to talk with her teachers and share your experience of how honoring your child's will in some circumstances has transformed your interactions from oppositional to respectful. You can also share how your attempt to honor your child's experience has led you to see new talents in her that you hadn't noticed before. Use some concrete examples to demonstrate for your child's teachers how they can practice reframing your child's oppositional behavior. Also share that you understand that the teacher needs to control and manage her classroom, and that you understand that certain behaviors are far outside the limits

and they need to be controlled. You can share with the teacher that simply honoring your child's perspective on a few occasions can be enough to convince your child that the teacher does see her perspective and is not simply just out to get her.

As a final note, you may reflect that this seems like a lot of work to do. You may find yourself wishing that you didn't have so much to do for your child. It may feel like you're being asked to try to change the whole educational system. In some respect, that is exactly what you are doing. Each parent who advocates for change may begin a general revisioning of what we want for our children's education. There are other models for teaching children other than placing the highest emphasis on conformity, compliance, and control. Parents can play a role in shaping the demand for a different vision. In helping your child to transform his problems into strengths, you may find yourself on the path of becoming a social activist.

SUPPORT YOUR CHILD'S SUCCESS

As you introduce some of these new exercises and your child begins to identify his own emotions and see them as sensitivity to others, you'll be able to notice your child engaging in new interpersonal interactions with you and others. Pay special attention to what your child is doing right. This will serve to not only reinforce or reward your child for transforming his behavior, but it will help you problem solve for other interpersonal difficulties.

Sometimes problems are simply the result of unfortunate learned behaviors. For example, if your child blurts out inappropriate comments that are socially uncomfortable, it may be because he finds the eye-popping, jaw-dropping reactions he gets from adults to be stimulating. Your child may be interpreting these visual cues as positive reinforcement. Remember that a big interpersonal gift of ADHD is that these children are tuned in to people's emotional reactions and attend more to nonverbal cues than what adults actually say.

Additionally, sometimes bad behavior can be easily managed by simple problem solving around conditions preceding such behavior. For example, Sharon found that her daughter, Frances, would bully her younger brother in the morning when they were getting ready for school. When asked to look for times when this behavior did not occur or when Frances was helpful toward her younger brother, Sharon began paying attention. One morning she noticed that things ran very smoothly, Frances didn't bully her brother, and the family was able to get out of the house without any major meltdowns. As Sharon drove her daughter to school, she expressed her appreciation and asked her what was different about this morning. Her daughter said that because it was picture day, they had spent the night before picking out her outfit and braiding her hair. When she woke up that morning, all she had to do was put on the outfit she had already picked out and eat. Frances explained that since she was all ready to go in the morning, she didn't mind her little brother following her around. She didn't have to worry about being late.

By catching her daughter doing something right and asking "What went right?" Sharon was able to change a long-standing interpersonal problem between her two children. Sharon had always thought that the morning tantrums and meltdowns were because her daughter had a medical disorder, ADHD, that made her act out. When Sharon went out of her way to catch her daughter doing something right, she uncovered the real cause of the morning meltdowns— her daughter had a lot on her mind, a lot to do, and she rightly perceived her little brother as getting in her way in the morning rush.

Paying attention when your child does something right leads to positive reinforcement, which is likely to increase the good behavior. But also, by asking "What went right?" you can solve specific problems and eliminate bad behavior. In Sharon's case, she changed the family routine so that either Sharon or her husband spent some time in the evening helping their daughter prepare for school the next day. They picked out clothes, they planned hairstyles, they packed backpacks, they even planned breakfast. In this way, Frances could get up in the morning without pressure and not feel bothered by her little brother. Sharon found that making this simple change dramatically transformed mornings in the home. By changing this one behavior Sharon saw how each behavior had a powerful chain reaction that escalated the tension in the home. When Frances was stressed out and trying to get ready, she would tease her little brother. Her little brother would cry, and Sharon would have to separate them and comfort her son. As Sharon quelled these fights, she became increasingly late and worried that she would not get to work on time. As she became more worried about work, she got mad at Frances for seeming to cause all these problems and putting this additional stress on the family. As Sharon got increasingly mad, Frances's bad behavior escalated because she was so sensitive to her mother's feelings, in this case anger. Francis usually acted out her mother's anger by hitting her brother. Once she hit her brother, a family meltdown was well on its way to happening.

Whereas before, it seemed like Frances was the sole cause of all the morning tension, on reflection, Sharon could see that the whole family's reactions led to a cycle that escalated the tension. By catching Frances doing something right, Sharon was able to turn this cycle around and stopped blaming Frances. This transformation for the whole family happened because Sharon had decided to pay attention to when things went right, to when Frances was not showing symptoms. By setting her mind in this way, Sharon was able to take advantage of a once-a-year event—the school photos—that changed the family routine in such a way that a major problem was serendipitously solved. Sharon's story illustrates not only the power of actively searching for your child doing something right, but also the power of the label of ADHD to affect your perception of him.

Because of this diagnosis, when the family has a breakdown and your child's interpersonal style results as a symptom, you are likely to identify your child's behavior as the cause of the family problems rather than a result. The diagnosis of ADHD, because it includes uncontrolled and impulsive behavior as a symptom, and because of the medical model, can make it seem like this behavior is driving negative family reactions. However, because of the interpersonal sensitivity of your child, it is often the case that his bad behavior is a reflection of the underlying, perhaps unexpressed interpersonal tensions in a situation. As the above example indicates, some significant tensions do not necessarily result from deep-seated interpersonal conflicts. Tensions may result from unfortunate family routines.

Additionally, by interpreting your child's behavior as the cause of, rather than a reflection of, family tensions, your sensitive child easily senses the blame he's subject to and internalizes an image of himself as bad. The more the diagnosis causes you to blame him for family tensions, even if you don't express it verbally, the more he will feel the blame and internalize it. And the more he blames himself, the more he tends to think of himself as bad and unable to control his behavior. The more he thinks of himself this way, the more his behavior will reflect this internal image.

EXERCISE: WHAT WENT RIGHT?

This whole dynamic of blame and bad behavior can be transformed by the following exercise:

1. Catch your child doing something right. Find a time when a bad behavior is not present or when a positive interaction is observed.

2. Ask yourself and your child, "What went right?" You will want to analyze the situation as much as possible. What was different? What preceded the good behavior? What followed the good behavior? Why were things different? Get as many details as possible.

3. Ask yourself in what ways is this bad behavior the reflection of family tensions rather than the cause of family tensions?

4. Make changes in family routines as appropriate. If this exercise reveals more deep-seated problems, seek counseling or outside help. For example, a child with ADHD may act out marital conflicts between the parents or unresolved depression and grief from one or both parents. It may be that therapy for one of the parents or marital therapy for both is needed to resolve an underlying conflict or tension that your child is reflecting back to you.

Summary

This chapter reviewed how symptoms of ADHD can be seen as an interpersonal gift. Children diagnosed with ADHD are very sensitive to the emotions of the people around them. They are prone to emotional contagion, or reflecting and acting out unexpressed emotions of people they feel connected to. This ability can lead to interpersonal disturbances, but it can be channeled to reveal and enhance your child's emotional sensitivity and deep connection with others.

CHAPTER 8

Your Exuberant Child: Reframing Hyperactivity

The symptom of hyperactivity is in some ways the easiest to reframe as a gift. As adults, how much would we pay to have more energy? Most adults suffer from a sort of hypoactivity disorder—not having enough energy. In a culture that is reporting skyrocketing rates of depression and a surge of disorders like chronic fatigue syndrome, it seems like there is no correct balance of energy. Either you have too much or too little.

What doctors and teachers call hyperactivity can also be called exuberance. Exuberance is characterized by high energy and an intense interest and curiosity in the world. Exuberant children are playful, intense, and can be fun to be around. Why does a trait that seems so obviously positive get turned into a disorder? As a parent of a child with this diagnosis, you are well aware that your child's excess of energy has demanded a lot of energy from you and her teachers. While the focus of this chapter will be on how to reframe this surplus of energy as a gift, it is worth considering, in passing, if the increasing rate in diagnosis of ADHD in children parallels the increasing rate of depression in the adult population? Both of these diagnoses are social judgments. If teachers and parents are reporting increasingly low levels of energy, then by comparison, our children may look like they are disordered in their high levels of energy.

Even so, it still remains that if your child has been diagnosed with ADHD, she likely shows higher levels of energy and activity compared to other children her same age. She is different from other children. This chapter will help you to increase your own and your child's appreciation for this high level of energy. You will learn two complementary strategies for helping you to manage your child. The first strategy will involve techniques to help your child contain her high level of energy so it isn't immediately and impulsively acted out. The second strategy involves finding ways to channel your child's energy in ways that reveal it as a resource rather than as a deficit.

APPRECIATION OF YOUR CHILD'S HIGH ENERGY

Imagine the following scenario: You come home on a Friday night after a full workweek. After preparing dinner for your family, you realize you have three more hours that you could use to work on your taxes, which are due in two months.

It's obvious from this scenario that having a lot of energy would be a good thing. Many of us come home from a long work week on a Friday and are tempted to order pizza because we're too tired to cook. After dinner, many of us just want to camp out in front of the TV for the rest of the night. As adults, the high level of activity depicted in the first scenario is so obviously beneficial, we have to ask, how did high levels of activity get characterized as a disorder in children?

One of the reasons it becomes a problem in children is because the high level of energy seemingly has a mind of its own. The high energy level is in the service of an unfolding urge or impulse felt by the child. It is not directed toward productive ends. The essential problem is that the energy is unfocused.

However, you can learn to view and help your child view the surplus of energy as a valuable resource. You can help your child be in charge of this energy, rather than being driven by it.

EXERCISE: TAKING OVER THE STEERING WHEEL

Many children with the diagnosis of ADHD describe their symptoms as being like having an internal motor that makes them go all the time. This exercise has two elements. In the first part, your child will practice becoming aware of and monitoring her internal "motor" activity. By becoming aware of it, she will be less likely to be driven by it. She will gain skills in noticing and tolerating the driven feeling. In the second part, your child will make fun cards with positive reminders that she can control herself and take charge of the energy.

To begin, talk to your child about how her excess energy can be thought of as a powerful motor that drives her. Ask her to draw a picture of the motor. Encourage her to talk about what the motor feels like and how fast it makes her go. Ask her before she goes to school to pay attention to the motor and just notice when it speeds up or slows down during the day.

After school, check in with your child and ask her what she noticed about the motor. Listen carefully as she tells you about her experience. Validate the power of the motor.

An exercise you can do even while driving home from school is to ask her to tell you about the motor inside. Some questions to ask are these:

- Where in your body do you feel the motor?

- How big is the motor?

- How fast is it?

- What color is it?

- When does the motor speed up?

- What happens before it speeds up?

- What happens after it speeds up?

- What happens when it speeds up?

- When does it slow down?

- What happens right before it slows down?

- What happens right after it slows down?

- What happens when it slows down?

Use some of your child's responses to suggest strategies for giving her control over the motor. For example, if your child says she notices the motor speed up when she sits next to her friend Tommy during reading group, you can suggest that she not sit next to Tommy during reading group, but that she can play with Tommy at recess. If she says she noticed her motor slow down when she was trying to fix one of the toys at school, suggest to her that when she finds her motor revving up out of control, she can find something to fix or tinker with. You can also suggest to her teacher that she be given certain responsibilities for projects such as tinkering with or setting up audiovisual equipment as a strategy for calming her down. You can also suggest to the teacher that he value and praise these activities and abilities displayed by your child. Similarly, at home you may want to offer a great deal of validation and approval for her exploring with and tinkering with mechanical objects. In this way, she can receive approval and a sense of self-worth for activities that are intrinsically rewarding to her. Often, gaining abstract knowledge from books will be a continual struggle for your child even when she becomes capable of high levels of achievement by using the strategies in this book. So it's important for your child to learn that practical projects that she finds easy and calming will also help her develop important skills.

Make a fun game out of creating cards that remind your child that she can control the motor. Tell her that she can notice when the motor revs up and take charge by imagining that she has her hands on the steering wheel and her feet on the brakes. For this exercise, you will need three-by-five or four-by-six index cards. You will use these to create vivid reminders for your child to help her control her energy. You can cut out and paste pictures of cars or boats on one side or have your child draw a car, boat, motor, or steering wheel on the front. On the other side, you can write out reminders for your child. Some examples of reminders follow:

- I can slow down the motor.

- I can steer the car.

- If I take a few deep breaths, I can put on the brakes.

- If I take time to feel the motor, I can take charge.

- I'm in charge.

- I can use this motor to help me pay attention.

- I can use this motor to help the teacher.

- I can use this motor to help other students.

- I can use this motor to do my homework.

- I can use this motor to clean my room.

- I know how to slow down the motor.

- I can put my hands on the steering wheel.

- I can sit still even if the motor is going fast.

- I can stay quiet by just noticing the motor.

Have your child take these cards to school. You can also keep them (or a second set) around the house as reminders of how to channel energy in positive ways. The more your child is involved in having fun in creating the cards, the more she'll be interested in looking at them and using them in school and other settings.

Ask your daughter to tell you stories about how and when she used the cards in school. Listen carefully and offer generous praise for using the cards and taking control of her behavior. You can help her problem solve if trouble arises. If she experiences other kids making fun of her cards, you can make suggestions about how she can handle the situation by standing up for herself or by using the cards in a way that won't draw the attention of other students.

This exercise combines some of the most fundamental cognitive behavioral strategies for transforming behavior. The first step is guiding your child in monitoring her behavior. Awareness generally precedes any change. By simply noticing the revved-up, driven feeling, your child will be taking a significant step toward gaining control. The more the driven feeling is in her awareness, the less she will impulsively act out. Additionally, by identifying antecedents and consequences of behavior, you can dramatically shape behavior.

Generally, you will want to make changes in your child's environment such that those situations that precede the motor slowing down occur more frequently. Similarly, you will want to change her environment to reduce or eliminate situations that cause her motor to speed up. Also, by asking your child to notice the consequences that follow the motor slowing down, she will begin to notice the subsequent rewards and may become more aware of the punishments when the motor speeds up. For example, it is likely that your child will report that one consequence of the motor speeding up is out-of-control behavior that gets negative responses from teachers and other students. By simply observing how these consequences follow from the speed of her internal motor, she will change her behavior to increase the frequency of positive responses.

You may want to record in your journal all the information you get over time from your child about what comes before, after, and during the motor speeding up and slowing down. After a few weeks of taking notes, you may want to summarize your findings by creating the following titles and listing underneath each title all the relevant behaviors.

- Behaviors That Slow the Motor Down

- Behaviors That Speed the Motor Up

- Consequences of Speeding the Motor Up

- Consequences of Slowing the Motor Down

Once you have a fairly long list of behaviors, you can shape your child's environment to help her manage her behavior. As a reminder, you will want to follow these two vital steps:

- Increase the activities or events that slow the motor down.

- Decrease or eliminate activities that speed the motor up.

Share with your child's teachers the information you've gathered to help your child manage her behavior while at school. You will also use the information about consequences of behavior to remind your child of the importance of paying attention to her inner motor. By reminding her of the negative consequences of a speeded-up motor and the positive consequences of a slowed-down motor, you will help her increase her motivation to exercise her control over the motor.

Finally, the cards will help remind your child in school and other settings that she can control her behavior. She may not be able to make the motor go away, but she can take charge and direct her own behavior. Positive self-statements can have powerful effects. Simply by suggesting to your child that she can sit still even if her motor is speeding up will help convince her that it's true.

Revving Down the Motor

In addition to creating an expectation in your child that she can control the motor, there are pretend games she can play to increase her chances of controlling it. The preceding exercise will provide powerful suggestions to your child that she is in charge. Just these suggestions and positive expectations can effect changes in your child's behavior. They are helpful in countering the message she may get from teachers and doctors that ADHD is impossible to control without medication. In addition to increasing her perception that she can begin to control her behavior, you can give her specific techniques for slowing down the motor.

Children live in the worlds of their imagination, and there is research showing that imagination can have powerful effects on feelings, thoughts, and even physical health problems (VanKuiken 2004). You can tap into your child's imagination in play to help her transform her life. Your child's imagination can become a powerful resource for containing and channeling her high levels of energy. Following are a few pretend games your child can try. Some of them she'll like, others she won't. You should try a few and only repeat the one that is most fun for your child. If it feels like a chore, your child won't be motivated to use it. If none of the games click with your child, try to make up your own images or pretend games that serve the same function.

EXERCISE: THE SPEEDOMETER

1. Tell your child you are going to play a pretend game in which she'll use her powers of imagination. Ask your child to sit down and take a few deep breaths. Then tell her to imagine a room that has a lot of dials and control valves. Or, if she prefers, she can imagine a cockpit of an airplane with all of its dials and switches. Invite her to playfully explore this control room. Ask her to find a speedometer that tells her how fast her motor is revving. Ask her to imagine that the speedometer goes from 0 to 100 miles an hour, then ask her to tell you what the speed is now. Tell your child that, just as you can move a thermostat to change the temperature in a room, she can change the speed of her motor by changing a powerful control valve. Tell her to imagine finding the control valve that determines the speed of the motor. When she finds it, ask her to slow down the motor speed. If she was at 50 miles per hour, tell her to move it to 20 miles per hour. Ask her how this level of energy feels. Then have her experiment until she finds a specific speed that feels comfortable—like she has enough energy to focus and pay attention but not so much that she can't sit still or feels like she is driven.

2. Practice this over and over, and remind her that she can use the control valve to change the speed of her motor. Remind her of her target speed, and tell her that she should use the

control valve to get to that speed whenever she feels she has too little or too much energy.

3. Spend some time playing with your child to make the control valve and speedometer more concrete. You can draw the room or cockpit where the speedometer and control valve are located. You can encourage her to draw both the speedometer and the control valve. If you can find any toys that have similar themes or objects, you can have her physically act out these control strategies.

4. Have her draw a speedometer on a blank four-by-six card with the needle pointed at the most comfortable speed for her internal motor. She can take this card and ones with different speeds to school as a reminder that she can control her energy level. You can also have her carry a card that has a picture or drawing of her control valve. On the other side of the card you can write, "I'm in charge!" Remind her to carry these with her to school.

EXERCISE: GAMMA RAY BURSTS

Children are often full of wonder about the universe, planets, and deep space. You can tap into this interest to help inspire them to work on focusing their intense energy. A particularly inspiring example is the recent discovery of gamma ray bursts, which are the brightest explosions since the big bang (Nadis 2004). Gamma ray bursts have the highest energy blasts yet found by astronomers, but what makes them particularly special is that the energy is not sprayed in all directions but is focused into narrow beams or jets. They are powerful, energetic bursts that are channeled like a laser beam. These most powerful of energy bursts found in the universe are caused by a star blowing up, and all of that energy gets funneled out into the universe in very focused jets.

Tell your child about this fascinating scientific discovery and let her know that she can be like a gamma ray burst by focusing her powerful energy like a laser beam. Tell her to imagine focusing her energy on whatever task is at hand or in school. For example, if she has worksheets to do for homework and has too much energy to sit still, remind her of the gamma ray burst. Tell her that right now her energy is like an explosion, with all the energy going off in every direction, but not able to accomplish anything. Tell her that she can focus her energy like the gamma ray burst and use it to get her homework done. You can have her draw pictures of what a gamma ray burst would look like and put it on a four-by-six card to take to school with her. On the other side of the card you can write, "I can focus my energy like a gamma ray burst." You might also want to track down the photos from the January 2004 issue of *Astronomy*. These photos can provide powerful images for your child, reminding her that she can control and focus her energy.

If you try these two pretend games and your child's interest is not piqued, work with her to develop an image or game that is fun for her. If she has a passionate interest in a sport, video game, or movie character, use her specialized interest to develop a game or visual image that will serve to help her channel and transform her high levels of energy.

REDIRECTING THIS POWERFUL RESOURCE

Even though your child's high level of energy can seem like a tremendous drain of your own energy, you can begin to think of it as a resource. It's important to remember that, while you can expect improvements in your child's control of her energy, by and large you cannot expect to get rid your child's high energy level and sense of being driven. If you keep this in mind, you will be more open to parenting strategies that will lead to improvements in your relationship with your child.

Staying Positive

A common mistake that parents with children diagnosed with ADHD make is to punish their child for bad behavior or academic failure by increasing the level of demands for quiet time or academic study. This doesn't work because your child's high energy is not willful—it is a reservoir that she needs to learn specific skills to manage. By punishing your child, you communicate that she is wrong rather than simply being different.

Another problem with using punishment with children diagnosed with ADHD is that most forms of punishment, while unpleasant for all children, are excruciating for children with ADHD. For example, sending a child to her room, prescribing quiet time, or taking away a favorite activity are more difficult for a child with ADHD to comply with. It is more difficult for a child with ADHD to stay quiet than for a child not so diagnosed. For this reason, she will likely appear to defy your demands for quiet time. This looks like defiance, which seems to warrant even more punishment, thus setting up yet another vicious cycle.

As a general rule, it is better to use positive reinforcement strategies for any child, but particularly for a child diagnosed with ADHD. One reason for this is that your child likely experiences rejection and failure at school and desperately needs a safe place at home where she can feel accepted for who she is. To the extent that you can eliminate punishment from your parenting repertoire, you will improve your relationship with your child and serve her more effectively.

Positive reinforcement means actively looking for positive behaviors or the absence of negative symptoms and offering praise and rewards. In short, you want to catch your child doing something right. This dramatic shift in parenting a difficult child can be hard, as you may have built up a lot of frustration and want to do what works most quickly. But it's important to remember the long-term toll that punishment takes on your child's self-esteem and sense of self-worth. While it may feel like a quick fix, punishment may lead to long-term aggravation of any existing behavior problems by reducing self-esteem.

Positive reinforcement takes more work from you as a parent, because you have to actively look for positive behaviors to reinforce. Additionally, it requires some thought and energy on your part to determine how you will offer praise or rewards. But the long-term payoffs are often positive. Positive reinforcement will improve your relationship with your child because she won't feel bad about herself or be angry with you for taking something she likes away from her.

The stronger your relationship with your child, the more "capital" you have for negotiating behavior change rather than enforcing it.

The Power of Responsibility

One of the more effective strategies for managing your child's behavior might be called "preventative behavioral management." Knowing what your child is good at and what she continually struggles with, you can begin to channel her energy in productive ways that will prevent behavioral problems from occurring. As an example, your child has a basic need to be active and to be engaged in some form of hands-on project, even more so than other children. You can use this to your advantage. Instead of punishing your child after a behavioral problem has occurred, you can prevent bad behavior through a simple strategy: giving your child responsibility for specific projects that are of interest to her and are helpful to you.

The first transformative principle of this strategy is that, by giving your child responsibility, you are conveying your trust and confidence in her. Rather than making her do household chores as a punishment for bad behavior, you can reframe certain tasks such that you are entrusting her with this project that would be of great benefit to the family. You may at times want to frame your request as a reward. For example, if you catch your child in good behavior, you can say that since she is showing so much improvement, you would like to give her the responsibility of a special project.

It is important to be thoughtful about what the project entails. You will want to match the project to something that your child might enjoy. As examples, you could give her something broken that could be fixed or at least tinkered with. As described in a previous chapter, children with ADHD tend to find being in nature calming. You might ask your child to do some landscaping or pulling weeds, which would be a good use of her high energy and interest in nature. You can begin to think of your child's high energy as a resource rather than as a deficit.

One reason this seemingly simple strategy has been overlooked is that our culture devalues these sorts of projects and considers them to be menial labor. In fact, many people love to fix broken objects, get their hands dirty, and use their hands and bodies to clean things up or improve the environment. The hyperemphasis on book learning and school achievement has led us to devalue all other activities, especially for our children. In this way, parents often use these sorts of tasks as punishment for bad behavior because they don't value these tasks.

However, a lot of these tasks can be more enjoyable for children with ADHD, who benefit greatly from sensuous engagement with the world. Children with ADHD often like to see something get solved or accomplished. In part, this is their frustration with schoolwork: it is abstract and seems unrelated to everyday life. As a parent you can take advantage of this frustration by directing your child's energy and intelligence toward solving real-life problems and improving the environment. But it is important as a parent that you convey respect for these tasks.

The second transformative principle of this strategy is that it channels her energy, keeping your child entertained and occupied in what will seem to her a meaningful activity. This will prevent her from getting in more trouble but will also be calming in itself. It is important to remember that, for your child, meaningful means seeing concrete results related to the sensory world. So activities that involve fixing objects or improving the environment through household chores or landscaping can be meaningful to your child if you frame them that way. It may be that these activities have a calming effect, giving your child more attention for schoolwork or other tasks requiring focused, abstract attention.

Following are two scenarios that contrast the use of punishment with the use of positive reinforcement and giving your child responsibility for household projects.

Scenario 1: Punishment

Robin tells you that she wants to go play baseball with some friends. You tell her no, saying that she will have to get ready because you will have to leave shortly to take her sister to an appointment. Robin starts crying and gets angry that she can't go play and has to get in the car. Her emotional display quickly turns into a full-blown tantrum with loud yelling. You raise your voice and tell Robin to control herself, but she doesn't. You tell her she has to calm down now or she will not get to watch TV that evening. She seems to lose even more control and cries even more loudly. Raising your voice, you tell her that she needs to get herself ready to leave the house and to get in the car. After many threats, she pulls herself together, still crying and sulking, and drags herself to the car. When you take your other daughter to the appointment, Robin runs around the waiting room and loudly asks you if she gets to watch TV that night. You say you will talk about it at home, and she whines louder and louder that you're being unfair.

That night, you tell her that instead of watching TV with the family she has to go to her room. While in her room she whines loudly that it's not fair, cries, and creates messes by throwing her toys around aggressively. Her father asks her to be quiet and reminds her that this is the consequence of her temper tantrum. Robin continues to complain loudly that it's not fair. Her father tells her that if she doesn't stop whining, she won't be able to watch TV the next night. Robin starts crying again and yelling that no one cares about her. After her father leaves, Robin starts thinking that something must be really wrong with her because she cannot control her behavior and both of her parents are mad at her. She feels very alone because she thinks her parents are mad at her. When they're angry, she doesn't feel like she can talk to them.

Scenario 2: Responsibility and Positive Reinforcement

Robin tells you that she wants to go play baseball with some friends. You tell her no, saying that she will have to get ready because you will have to leave shortly to take her sister to an appointment. Robin starts crying and gets angry that she can't go play and has to get in the car. Her emotional display quickly turns into a full-blown tantrum with loud yelling. You walk away without giving her any attention while she has a tantrum. After a few minutes of crying and yelling, Robin realizes no one is paying any attention to her. She sees that you are rushing around looking for something. She says, "What are you looking for, Mommy?" You tell her you cannot find the keys. She runs around the house looking for the keys and finds them for you. When she gives you the keys, you say to her, "Thank you so much Robin. Whew! You're a lifesaver. You have been so helpful. You're doing such a great job helping me out and helping all of us get your sister to her appointment on time." In the car on the way to the appointment, you say to Robin, "Since I can see you're trying so hard to be good and help out the family, I want to give you responsibility for working on a project. I want you and your dad to work together to make something to hold all the family keys so we won't lose them so easily." Robin gets really excited about the idea and starts telling you all the ideas she has for how to make a key holder to hang in the front hallway. While you're in the waiting room for her sister's appointment, Robin keeps talking about all the things she will have to buy with Dad to make the key holder and how she is going to make it.

That night when her father comes home, Robin excitedly tells him about the keyholder that Mom said she could help him make. She tells her dad about all of her different ideas. Dad tells her that if she does some of her worksheets for school after dinner, they can run to the hardware store to get some of the material for the key holder. Robin jumps up and down because she is so excited to go to the hardware store. She says she will do her worksheets so she can go to the store to pick out the stuff.

How the Strategies Compare

As you can see, the difference between punishment and positive reinforcement has dramatic consequences for your child's behavior and your relationship with her. In the examples above, when the mom chose to ignore the temper tantrum, she was taking away one reinforcer for such behavior. Sometimes the attention that children get for this behavior actually reinforces it. It may be that by throwing a temper tantrum your child successfully takes your attention away from something else and puts it back on herself. Although your attention in such cases is negative, it may be experienced as rewarding for a child. Children can often bounce back from a temper tantrum quickly if it doesn't receive any attention. Additionally, over time temper tantrums will be less likely to occur if they are not given attention. Of course you want to ensure your child's physical safety and make sure that she doesn't engage in any behaviors that could hurt herself or others.

More important than not reinforcing bad behavior is offering positive reinforcements for good behavior. This will not only increase the good behavior, but will increase your child's sense of self-worth and connection to you. If your child feels that you value her, she will be more likely to feel she can share her thoughts and feelings with you. The more she can share with you, the stronger your relationship will be. The strength of your relationship with your child is the single most powerful protective factor for preventing bad behavior.

Also notable in the above scenarios is that by offering the child a project to work on, she had another avenue for connecting with her father. She was able to channel her high energy into excitement and planning the new project. Rather than tearing up the doctor's waiting room, she could excitedly plan for his new project. Your child will feel a sense of self-esteem and a need to live up to the responsibility you have offered.

Summary

This chapter reviewed the way in which symptoms of hyperactivity can be seen as a valuable resource. If your child can learn to focus her high levels of energy, she can use the very same symptom to fuel productive accomplishment. Your child's energy can make her exuberant, charismatic, and fun to be around. By following the techniques in this chapter, this high energy level can be transformed so that she can use it to achieve her goals.

CHAPTER 9

Your Emotionally Expressive Child

EXQUISITE SENSITIVITY

One of the symptoms parents of children with ADHD struggle with most is their child's emotional outbursts. Parents may cringe inside and dread social situations where they expect their child to throw a temper tantrum. Children with ADHD have little emotional control. When they're sad, they are given to fits, when they're angry, they are given to tantrums, and when they are excited they're prone to acting like a Tasmanian devil, whirling around and leaving big messes as they go. Not only are they prone to big displays of emotion, they seem to be subject to a more frequent loss of emotional control than other children.

These very same symptoms that parents may have come to dread also represent a remarkable gift: emotional sensitivity and intensity. Your child may be prone to more frequent emotional reactions because he is so responsive and sensitive to life, to other people, and to monitoring his connection with others. It is like children with ADHD go through each day living in a world that has the volume turned up much higher than for others. This quality of emotional sensitivity may be seen as the fundamental difference that constitutes ADHD and can be seen as what, in part, drives the other gifts of ADHD.

The gift of emotional sensitivity is directly related to the gift of interpersonal intuition. Our interpersonal relationships and sense of connection to others depend on emotional sensitivity. We connect with others by understanding how they feel. Remember how President Bill Clinton moved a nation by saying "I feel your pain"? Children with ADHD have this same capacity. We connect with others by sharing our feelings. The more emotionally sensitive a child is, the more he can empathize with others because he has felt those same emotions. Our capacity to connect, be moved by another person, and offer empathy depend on our emotional sensitivity. Your child has this gift in abundance.

The gift of emotional sensitivity is also directly related to the gift of creativity. Because the world impinges on your child more deeply, his capacity to represent the world in artistic ways is increased. He can see things others cannot see and feel things that others just barely notice. His perception of the world strikes us as creative because it is different. Poet Rainer Maria Rilke, in describing a powerful spiritual experience, wrote that "everything penetrates more deeply within me, and no longer stops at the place, where until now, it always used to finish" (Franquemont 1999, 98). It is similar with your ADHD child. Note how in the quote above, this capacity is presented as a much sought after quality. This experience of having the world impinge deeply is how your child experiences the world on a day-to-day basis.

The gift of intense emotional experience also fuels your child's deep connection to the natural and organic world. Whereas for many adults, the natural world is merely part of the background, the child diagnosed with ADHD is intensely sensitive to the organic, growing, alive, nurturing qualities of the natural world. Your child's ecological consciousness is related to a sensitivity and concern about his environment. Because the volume is turned up on the world, your child can feel attuned to plants, animals, trees, and other aspects of the natural landscape. As noted in chapter 6, this capacity is much needed in the world today to help work toward conservation and preservation of natural resources.

Emotional expressivity is also directly related to your child's surplus of energy. His intense emotions are like a high-powered fuel driving his behavior and compelling him to give behavioral expression to his intense experiences. Hyperactivity is a behavioral strategy for discharging high levels of emotional experiences. As a child, it's hard to sit still and focus attention with such powerful emotions coursing through one's body and mind.

EMOTIONAL SENSITIVITY AND EMOTIONAL EXPRESSION

Part of transforming emotional intensity from a symptom into a gift is helping your child separate emotional sensitivity from emotional expression. There is an automatic quality to your child's behavior, an impulse immediately followed by behavior. Control of emotions is weak in all children compared to adults because the part of the brain that exerts such control is still developing. So the capacity to control emotions is a skill all children must learn. A child diagnosed with ADHD shares this lack of control, but it's paired with emotional experience on a much greater magnitude than in other children. The intense emotion for a child with ADHD typically does not enter awareness—it gets acted out impulsively and discharged.

While this chapter will offer an exercise for reining in emotional sensitivity, the emphasis will be on breaking the automatic nature of intense emotion followed by intense emotional outburst. Your child will learn how to maintain his sensitivity without disrupting the environment with intense displays of emotion.

EXERCISE: HELPING YOUR CHILD ASK FOR HELP

In this exercise, the goal is simply to increase your child's awareness of the difficulty of managing his emotions. By increasing his awareness of his struggle, he can be guided to ask for help. By asking for help, your child will increase his chances of channeling his intense emotions in socially appropriate ways. Because every social situation is singular, there are no simple formulas to offer your child to help develop social skills. Also, by offering your child simplified, pat strategies, you tend to invalidate his sense of the intensity of his own reactions.

The most important aspect of the following exercise is that it reminds your child to put one step between emotional expression and emotional outburst. By directing your child to ask for help, you're offering him a strategy for breaking the automaticity in a way that seems reasonable to your child. By guiding him to ask for help, you are acknowledging that the intensity of his emotions may prevent him from rationally deciding how to effectively channel his sensitivity. And while you're validating him, you are also giving him one manageable step to insert between a strong emotion and a socially inappropriate behavior. One step between the emotion and action may be all that it takes to break the pattern of disruptive behavior.

Start by talking your child about his emotional intensity and reframing it for him as a gift. Give many examples of how emotional sensitivity is a much-needed trait in the world. Some examples might be these:

- Emotional sensitivity helps us to connect with others by showing them we know what they are feeling.

- Emotional sensitivity helps us see parts of the world that need to be fixed.

- It helps us see people that need our attention.

- It helps us know our own selves.

- It can lead to creativity.

- It helps you to care for other people.

Talk to your child about how there is a difference between our strong feelings and our behavior. Let him know that you can feel something strongly and not act it out in ways that disrupt others. Tell him that because he is so gifted with emotional sensitivity, he may need to ask for help from other adults to find ways of expressing his emotions in positive ways. Tell your child that whenever he feels a strong emotion that begins to feel uncontrollable, he should ask an adult (his teacher at school, you, or his other parent) to help him with it.

For one week, practice this with him at home. Whenever you notice him getting highly emotional, remind him to ask for help. If you catch him after his behavior has gotten out of control, rather than getting mad at him, remind him that next time, he can ask for help before he loses control. Reassure him that he does not have to figure out how to control himself. All that he has to do is ask for assistance.

After practicing for a week, ask your son to practice this at school. You will want to let his teachers know what you're working on. You may want to share with the teachers some specific strategies you discovered in your weeklong trial period for helping your child manage his intense emotions.

When your child is in a positive and calm frame of mind, ask him the following questions and write his responses in a journal.

- What can you do to help yourself when your emotions start to feel too big for you?

- What can we (your parents) do to help you when your emotions start to feel too big?

- What can your teachers do to help you when your emotions start to feel too big?

- What can your brother and sister do to help you when your emotions start to feel too big?

- What can your friends and classmates do to help you when your emotions start to feel too big?

Begin to try some of the suggestions your child comes up with. Guide your child to ask for the aid that he identified as being what he would most like. For one week, let your child practice asking for help, specifically the kind of help he wants. For example, your child might tell you that when he asks you for help when he gets mad at his little brother, he wants you to not only separate him and his brother physically, but he wants you to show that you understand why he is mad. Because of the diagnosis of ADHD, sometimes parents just assume that bad behavior is not rooted in a realistic complaint. The next time your child gets mad and asks for help, you might separate him and his brother and reassure him that you can see why he gets frustrated at his brother when he seems to get all the attention.

In trying this exercise, you can expect to transform your child's behavior just by guiding him to insert one behavior—asking for help—between his intense emotion and his impulsive action. In this way, you are not repressing your child's sensitivity, but helping him to gain social skills in one social situation after another. As he learns to get help, he will gradually gain the skills and strategies he needs to stay connected to his own gifted emotional life without disrupting the environment.

Often you will find that the more you validate the intense emotion your child feels, the more he'll be able to gain control. Any time you can immediately validate the feeling while channeling its expression, you can defuse a potential outburst. It is paradoxical that the more you negate, criticize, or deny your child's feeling, the more it will grow out of control. The more you validate it, the smaller it will get. You'll be amazed at the power of this one technique. For example, if your child is jealous, you will help him to gain control by deeply affirming his feelings: "Of course you want more of the attention that your little brother gets now. It's okay if sometimes you feel mad at him when Mommy's nursing him. But remember to ask me for help when you're mad rather than jumping up on Mommy when she nurses your little brother." In this way, you do not make him feel like he is a bad person for having his feelings. The worse he feels about himself, the more his behavior is likely to be disruptive. The more he sees his feelings as acceptable, the more he will be motivated to work with you to help manage them.

SURFING THE WAVES OF FEELINGS

The next exercise will help your child use the image of surfing, a fun and exciting sport, to help him manage his emotional sensitivity. He will learn how to go with the flow of his emotions. By doing this he will avoid two pitfalls of managing emotions: resistance and outbursts. A common mistake in dealing with emotions is trying to teach your child to resist his emotions through effort or willpower. These strategies often backfire. The more your child tries to resist a powerful emotion, the more likely he is to lose control. Resistance tends to make the emotion grow stronger and more primitive. Throw on top of that a feeling of failing to control the emotion, and resistance becomes like fuel to a fire.

The Problem with Resistance

One common strategy parents use in trying to get their child to resist an emotion is to frame emotional outbursts as a moral failing. Parents may be tempted to tell a child that failure to control emotions is bad behavior that is morally wrong because it's defiant. This strategy will likely backfire, because the more you make your child feel wrong, the more negative emotions will pile up and the more unmanageable his emotions will become. One model for understanding this is the "container model" (Honos-Webb et al. 2001). According to this model, you can think of each person as having a container that allows them to hold a certain amount of emotional experience. If too many or too powerful emotions fill the container, the person can no longer hold them, and a breakdown of sorts occurs. In children, this breakdown looks like a temper tantrum. So if your child is already struggling with a powerful negative emotion, for example, jealousy of a brother, and you tell him that the emotion is bad, he then has to contain both being jealous of his brother and feeling bad about having the emotion and feeling misunderstood. This is a recipe for a behavioral breakdown.

The container model has important implications for understanding your child. A child's container is much smaller than an adult's. This means that behavior that would be terrible for an adult is often actually appropriate for a child. Not only is the child's container smaller—meaning that he has less capacity for tolerating emotions—but his brain is less developed. He cannot understand the world as well as an adult can, so he is often more prone to being frustrated and experiencing negative emotion. Consider the following example. You go to the store with your son Mark. Mark finds a thick science fiction book, which he pulls off the shelf and brings to you to buy for him. You know that the book is far beyond his reading capacity and that even if he could read it he wouldn't be interested in the subject matter. You tell him that the book is not appropriate for him and that you won't buy it for him. You point out that he has already picked out a book and let him know that if he wants more you plan to go to the library the next day, where he can get as many books as he wants. Mark starts to cry, saying that he wants this book and needs it now. As you remain firm, Mark throws himself on the ground and has a temper tantrum, embarrassing you in the process.

Depending on how old your child is, this behavior may be perfectly predictable. For a younger child, the disappointment at not getting what he wants can feel enormous. In addition, because his brain is not fully developed, he does not have as much capacity to hold back his emotional expression. On top of that, he isn't able to fully understand your logic that he would not really enjoy or even use the book. His disappointment and frustration may be more than he can contain. As a parent, it is absolutely right to persist in being firm by not buying the book. Over time these disappointments serve to expand your child's capacity to contain disappointment. Not only are there real limits to what you can provide your child with, but he actually needs disappointments in order to build his capacity to tolerate future disappointments.

The mistake parents often make is getting mad at a child because his reactions are so immature. Children *are* immature, and acting in the way described above is predictable for young children. The struggle for you as a parent is to increase your own capacity to tolerate your child's temper tantrums without becoming punishing because of social embarrassment. Remember that, because of your child's interpersonal and emotional sensitivity, the more angry you become, the more your child will likely be highly attuned to your emotional state. This sensitivity is more likely to bust his container, literally creating an outburst. Many parents manage tantrums and outbursts by punishing their child or giving in to the child. Both of these parental behaviors are likely to increase the child's tendency toward more frequent and larger outbursts. The more he is punished, the worse he will feel about herself. This will fill up his container with bad feelings, making him incapable of tolerating other distressing emotions. This intolerance extends to even small disappointments like the one described above. The more you give in to a temper tantrum, the less opportunity your child has to increase his capacity to tolerate disappointment and other negative emotions.

The Problem with Outbursts

When helping your child manage his emotions, the second pitfall to avoid is allowing him to discharge his negative emotions by acting out in a disruptive way. As a parent, it's important to recognize that while you don't want to facilitate your child in resisting powerful emotion, neither do you want to facilitate negative behavior. You don't want to punish your child for outbursts, but you do want to direct him to more appropriate strategies for coping with intense emotions. The exercise below provides one such strategy that can serve as preventative medicine. It will help decrease the likelihood that your child will see only two options for dealing with emotions: repress or act out. You will want to model a third strategy that will serve him for the rest of his life: staying with the emotion without acting it out.

EXERCISE: STAY WITH THE EMOTION

Ask your child to play a pretend game with him that will help him with his powerful emotions. You will want to start by telling him (or reminding him) that his ADHD means that he has a special gift of emotional sensitivity. Tell him that he is different from others because he feels things more intensely, but that this is a gift. Tell him to think of how you can use the volume knob to turn the sound up or down on a TV or radio. Tell him that he is like a radio where the volume is turned up higher, so he is more in tune with and more sensitive to the world and other people.

Tell him that he needs to have special skills to manage his emotions so he can fit in at school and not get in trouble. Tell him that, like the superheroes that have special abilities, he may sometimes struggle to fit in and need to develop strategies for getting along with others. Tell him that you will practice a pretend game to help him with this task.

Let him know that the name of the game is "Surfing the Waves of Emotion." In this game he pretends like his emotions are waves. Tell him that, like waves, emotions tend to get bigger and bigger and then, right as they peak, they start to get smaller. Tell him to imagine his powerful emotions as waves and picture himself surfing a big wave. He can plan on the wave getting bigger, but if he just hangs on it will start to get smaller all by itself. He doesn't need to do anything; he just needs to imagine surfing a wave.

Now you can try the exercise. Have him think of an emotion he recently felt strongly. Ask him to bring the feeling back, feeling it almost as strongly as he did then. Tell him to take a few deep breaths and to relax.

Next, ask him to pay attention to the emotion he's feeling. As it gets stronger, tell him to imagine surfing the wave of the emotion. This means that like a surfer he stays with the wave and rides it out. Remind him to stick with the feeling and not try to jump away from it.

Practice this with him daily on smaller, more manageable emotions. Tell him that like a surfer, you have to learn on the smaller waves. Practicing on the smaller waves will help with the bigger waves, but the real test will come when the big waves come. Talk to him about how he can remember to practice this when he is in school or when the waves seem really big. Develop strategies for him to remember to try surfing his emotions in other settings.

Spend some time creating playful reminder cards. Get blank four-by-six cards. From magazines, cut out photos of surfers, surfboards, big waves, or other images that evoke surfing. Paste these on one side of the blank cards. You can also let your child draw colorful pictures of waves, surfers, and surfboards. On the other side of the card, write a reminder affirmation. Here are some examples:

- Surf the wave.

- Stay with the feeling.

- Watch the wave get bigger.

- At the highest point, the wave will get smaller.

- Take a deep breath.

- Ride out the wave.

- You can surf the feeling.

- You can stay in control.

Keep track of how your child is using these strategies at school. Talk to him about when it seems to work and when it doesn't. Help him problem solve if there are specific obstacles. Remind him that they key to becoming a world-class surfer is "practice, practice, practice." Tell him not to get discouraged if it doesn't always work. Tell him that even the best surfers wipe out on big waves and that he will get better with practice.

THE CANARY IN THE COAL MINE

You may have become discouraged about your child's negativism toward school. You may be surprised to learn that scholars of education also show a negative attitude toward the current educational system and are calling for sweeping changes.

It has been argued that the current education system is an outdated model based on the industrial revolution. By analogy, children are like products and schools are like assembly lines that do not vary in how each product is assembled. The model has not accommodated the recent technological revolution in our culture and hasn't accommodated the unique needs of individual students. As one scholar, Chris Yapp, argues, "Education is the last model of Fordism—you put children on a conveyor belt at the age of four and let them fall off at different stages. From a quality viewpoint, they fall off at the point at which they fail. But you can choose your car, so why can't you have millions of national curriculums? Why not have a curriculum that meets the needs of each child?" (Fulton 1997, 69).

Even with the advent of the digital age, the current education system has not fully taken advantage of the many possibilities that technologies offer for transforming the way students learn. One model has suggested that students could use current technologies and Internet resources to direct their own content areas and to gain technical expertise necessary for operating in a digital world. The model based on the industrial revolution currently is failing to meet the needs of students and failing to take advantage of staggering technological innovations that offer the promise of transforming the way students learn.

One scholar, Professor Brent Davies, envisions a future in which children could do independent learning either in a school technology center or even at home (Fulton 1997). He argues that technologies such as the Internet, video conferencing, and educational software programs would allow for a comprehensive school program that would not require students to go to school five days a week. He also suggests that taking full advantage of technological innovation would reduce the burden on teachers who currently are underpaid and whose needs are not respected, as evidenced by overcrowded classrooms without adequate resources due to budgetary constraints. Similarly, Chris Yapp has challenged our current expectations of teachers to be "guard, nanny, subject expert and administrator" (Fulton 1997, 69). As mentioned earlier, recent research has demonstrated that teachers are in part responsible for the increased rates of diagnosis of ADHD (Sax and Kautz 2003). Given the unrealistic demands and expectations put on teachers, it should come as no surprise that they are eager to find quick solutions to the problems wrought by children whose behavior is disruptive to class.

The purpose of this review of the current failings of the education system is to validate that your child's criticism of school is shared by forward-looking scholars. Your child's complaints may not be a symptom of being disordered, but rather a very perceptive summary of the current failings of an out-moded education system. All of this reflects on your child's emotional sensitivity.

The metaphor of the canary in the coal mine refers to miners using a canary when they were working in mines as a gauge of oxygen levels. Because canaries are more sensitive, they would die if there wasn't enough oxygen. When the canary died, the miners knew it was time to leave the mine. This metaphor relates to ADHD, because given the current call for sweeping reform in the education system, your child's difficulties in school may be seen as a warning sign not of your child's problems, but of the failings of the education system.

The purpose of offering you, as a parent of a child with ADHD, this metaphor is to help you to value your child's stance toward school. It does not mean that you need to say, "Yeah, the education system is a mess, and it's all the teacher's fault that my child is struggling." However, it may give you a certain appreciation for your child's cogent perceptions of the school system and a sense that he really is not getting his needs met. As a parent, there are several strategies you can take in handling your child's complaints.

Honoring Your Child's Complaints

One strategy is to avoid devaluing your child's complaints that his needs are not being met. In fact, you might want to encourage him to elaborate on his complaints. But rather than framing them just as complaints, ask him to identify how his needs are not being met at school. You will want him to see how seriously you are taking his concerns, and you might want to get out a notebook and start writing down what your child says isn't working. Some predictable complaints might be like the following:

- The teacher is boring.

- I get in trouble for not sitting still.

- Nothing I learn has anything to do with the real world.

- Classes are boring.

- I'm more interested in other subjects.

- I want to play with the computers more.

- The worksheets are too much work.

- I get in trouble when I talk to other kids.

- I can't get help when I don't understand.

■   School days are too long.

As you can see from this list, many of your child's complaints are similar to the demands for change that are being called for by scholars. Rather than getting mad at your child for not adapting to an outdated system, you can honor his complaints and then start to problem solve about how to get his needs met.

How to Get Your Child's Needs Met

Once you have the list of your child's unmet needs, begin to talk to him about what could be done to meet them. Let him talk about how he would solve the problem. He might come up with some creative ideas that you can take action on. He might realize that, with so many students and one teacher, it will be difficult to get every need met. What is important in this step is that you show your child that you honor his needs and complaints. In this way, you're not attributing his problems to his diagnosis, and you can reframe for him the importance of his own experience.

Become an Education Reformer

As a parent, you probably haven't thought of yourself as needing to become an activist just to see that your child receives the education he deserves. However, the next step may be to make a list of a few of your child's legitimate complaints and to consider presenting these concerns to your child's teachers and principals. You can use many of the strategies you learned in chapter 4 on how to become your child's advocate rather than his apologist.

Like evolutionary mutations that are naturally selected for and help a species to survive, your child's intense sensitivity may help teachers and school administrators to recognize the dramatic changes that need to happen in the education system. Some of the changes that were mentioned earlier actually have the potential to save resources. For example, allowing children to have self-directed learning sessions where they use computer and Internet resources to explore individualized topics of their own interest would meet the needs of both children and teachers. Students could explore their own interests and teachers could have a break from trying to keep the attention of a large group of children on one topic.

In the next chapter we will discuss some alternatives to a standard public school education. If your child is not succeeding and is in a setting that won't accommodate his unique gifts, you may want to consider an alternative educational setting. However, your child's sensitivity may give you an opportunity to work for change in the setting that needs to be changed—the traditional public schools.

Encouraging your child to join you in your crusade to transform the educational system can help transform his problem behaviors into a gift. His creativity and impatience can be fuel to generate ideas for changing the system. For example, he may propose fund-raisers to get more computers in school or suggest field trips to high-tech museums. His energy might be contagious to you and others.

KEEP THE CONNECTION

The most important benefit that will result from seeing your child as an intensely gifted and sensitive agent for change is the connection it will forge with him. Even if you don't succeed in making any changes in the structure of his education, you will succeed in showing him that you value his way of seeing the world. This is the single most important element in transforming your child's symptoms into gifts.

The main reason that children who are diagnosed with ADHD become increasingly difficult in school and home settings is because their symptoms separate them from their parents. You can change this easily. If you emphasize connection over compliance, you can radically transform your child. More than anything, your child needs you. While it is perfectly predictable that parents will get angry and frustrated with children who won't comply, you have to remember that though it seems your child is pushing you away, he needs you to stay connected to him even in the face of his increasing independence.

It may help you to realize that your child's connection to you is not at all the same thing as compliance. Sometimes defiance can be a sign of self-reliance, and you can paradoxically stay connected to your child by honoring his self-reliance. It seems like a paradox, but the more you honor his self-reliance, the more you connect to him because you're accepting him for who he is rather than trying to change him. A further paradox is that the more you honor your child's unique perceptions of the world, the more he will honor your need to set limits.

Out of all the exercises and strategies presented throughout this book, the most important strategy for you as a parent is to stay connected to your child. The more you can find a way to honor his differences, the more his behavior will be transformed. Children with ADHD get many complaints about their behavior, and it can be confusing. Some of their behavior simply represents their difference. Some of their behavior truly is inappropriate or defiant. Different behavior becomes bad behavior when children feel that they are being punished or feel disconnected from their parents. You may not always be sure when the behavior has crossed the line from different to bad. In either case, whether in validating your child's perceptions or setting limits, the more you can stay connected, the more you will decrease bad behavior and increase his willingness to honor your perceptions and needs.

Summary

This chapter reviewed that way in which symptoms of ADHD can be seen as a form of intense emotional sensitivity. Your child's sensitivity can be seen as a gift, increasing his capacity to create and to connect with others. One strategy for helping your child preserve his sensitivity and maintain socially appropriate behavior is to encourage him to ask for help when he finds his emotions getting out of control. This strategy gives your child permission to admit that he cannot control his emotions while giving him a technique for learning on-the-spot methods for effectively handling social situations. The chapter also offered specific techniques for monitoring and managing emotions as they emerge.

CHAPTER 10

How to Navigate Educational and Mental-Health Systems

As a parent of a child with ADHD, you may feel yourself heartened by the new perspective you have gained on your child. You might be feeling that you have thought your child was uniquely gifted but unappreciated all along. You may have found yourself charmed by your child at times, and at other times you thought that her behavior was part of her ADHD symptoms. You may have even hidden your affection for your child's irreverence, fearing that you might encourage bad behavior.

The main point of this book can be summarized into two major principles:

■   Your positive perceptions of your child will transform her.

■   Your close connection with your child will transform her.

Because your child is so sensitive and interpersonally intuitive, she knows exactly how you are evaluating her. You cannot hide your feelings from her. She is particularly attuned to how you are reacting to her. The more you can view her in positive ways, the more she will internalize that perception and act it out. The power of the self-fulfilling prophesy cannot be underestimated.

This power means that what you expect from your child will create those very same qualities. Research has demonstrated that teachers' expectations for students' performance came to have powerful effects in creating the behavior they expected to see (Rosenthal 1987). This phenomenon is much more powerful for parents and children. The good news is that your expectations for your child have a lot of power to transform her. The bad news is, you can't fake it. Your child is sensitive and will pick up any insincerity.

The premise of this book, that your child has a difference that is a gift and not a disorder, has the power to transform her life. You need only to convey this powerful expectation to your child, and she will absorb it like a sponge. As your expectations change, so will your ability to connect with your child. The more you connect with your child, the more dramatic a transformation you can expect to see.

When children with ADHD behave badly, it is usually because they feel badly about themselves and because they are angry that they are not feeling loved unconditionally by their parents. Children with ADHD feel poorly about themselves in part because of the extreme emphasis on school achievement over all other talents and interests. One psychologist attributes the high rates of depression that accompany learning disorders to this emphasis: "In our modern technological society, where education is more important and more highly valued than ever, academic achievement and school-related intelligence have attained an importance that is probably far greater than ever before" (Migden 2002, 155).

By conveying to your child that the label of ADHD means she has a gift, you can turn around both of these causes of bad behavior. As your child learns to value her difference, she will not need to act out her sense of inferiority or frustration. Also, if you can maintain your sense of closeness with your child, even in the face of apparently bad behavior, your child will no longer need to act out her sense of being alienated.

Just by transforming your vision of your child from disordered to gifted, you can facilitate a dramatic transformation. While it is predictable that parents of children with ADHD will at times feel anger, impatience, and frustration with their child, you can channel these feelings toward the culture's intolerance of your child's gift. You yourself can be transformed into a social activist as you become aware of how your child has been in some ways oppressed by the current medical model and a failing educational system.

COPING WITH THE REST OF THE WORLD

As you come to appreciate your child's gifts, you may find yourself continually frustrated by the lack of validation of your new perspective in the real world. There are three strategies for coping with others' attitudes toward your child. One is to transform your own negative emotional responses toward others' rejecting attitudes. A second is to become an advocate for your child in mental-health and educational settings. A final approach is to find alternative treatments and educational settings that respect your child's difference as a gift.

One thing all of these strategies have in common is that, as a parent, you remain active in your efforts to cope with your child's diagnosis of ADHD. The worst thing you can do is to give up and give in to feeling hopeless and helpless. This passive reaction has the potential to lead to depression. Recent research has found that children diagnosed with ADHD have a poorer response to medication when their primary care provider reports depressive symptoms. These researchers conclude that "[o]ur findings suggest that consideration of parental psychological adjustment may be key when treating children with medication. Initial screening of parents for depressive symptoms, followed by treatment for those who are at least mildly depressed, might result in more children with ADHD showing excellent response to treatments that are medication based" (Owens et al. 2003, 549).

These findings suggest that when you feel hopeless, it is important for you and for your child's recovery that you seek treatment for yourself. But these findings indicate a powerful truth about your child's symptoms: your own level of functioning dramatically affects your child's symptoms. However, by remaining active in your coping efforts, you have the power to prevent depression.

Transform Your Feelings

While it is predictable that at times you will feel hopeless, help-less, angry, frustrated, and filled with despair, it is also important that you find effective strategies for coping with these feelings. As you do with your child, it is important that you validate and honor these feel-ings, but that you do not become overwhelmed by them. You can try the exercise in chapter 9 called "Stay with the Emotion" with your own feelings about your child's behavior and diagnosis. For example, if you have to face yet another teacher making complaints about your child's behavior in class, you may feel a sense of despair clouding your mind. As discussed in relation to your child in chapter 9, you don't want to repress the feeling and pretend everything is okay. Neither do you want to just give in to it, go to bed, and pull the covers over your head. You, too, can surf it out. You will find that as you allow yourself to feel the despair and let it peak in intensity, it will subside.

If you feel any despair or hopelessness to its full power, you will find that the experience not only lessens but transforms into a radi-cally different experience. Psychologist Alvin Mahrer calls this trans-formation of fully experienced emotion, "the deeper potential of experiencing" (Mahrer 2004). As an example, if you enter fully into your despair, you may find yourself focusing on the teacher's menac-ing tone as he seems to hurl thinly veiled threats and insults your way about your child's behavior. In this scene, the deeper potential for experiencing would be the menacing approach of the teacher. You can transform your despair by entering into your feeling of the teacher being menacing and becoming that menacing feeling yourself. The more you identify with this menacing feeling, the better you can transform your own sense of hopelessness to activation as you feel you have the power to intimidate others. That doesn't mean you will want to intimidate and menace other people in real life, but that you can use this newfound sense of power to make changes in your life and your child's life.

EXERCISE: FROM DESPAIRING
TO EMPOWERED

This exercise is inspired by *The Complete Guide to Experiential Psycho-therapy* (Mahrer 2004).

1. Identify a time when you are feeling hopeless or helpless. Typically, you may respond to this feeling by trying to distract yourself from it or push it away. In contrast to that, try to amplify the feeling by making it stronger and more intense. For example, you can allow the feeling of helplessness to turn into a complete feeling of paralysis and the hopelessness to turn into a feeling of complete doom and gloom.

2. As the feeling becomes more intense, try to find a specific memory or image that caused it. For example, it might have been when you got another complaining call from the teacher, and you found yourself dwelling on the image you had of the teacher sneering at you on the other end of the phone line and thinking you are the worst parent in the world. Of course, the teacher may not have been sneering or thinking that, but if you have an image of it, it can be healing to work with it.

3. Now imagine that you are the teacher. Try to feel the teacher's position of power and a menacing attitude toward you. Amplify your feeling that the teacher has the authority to pass judgments. Make the teacher's feelings stronger. The teacher may be all-powerful, the one who knows, the one who has the right to tell you how to understand your child. Follow your imagination in elaborating on this role.

4. Take this new feeling of being menacing, threatening, or empowered, and own it for yourself. Practice feeling like you are the judge. You can turn it around and tell the teacher that she is failing your child. Imagine telling the teacher that she is not serving the best interests of your child and that she does not even understand your child. Practice owning this feeling of power and authority. You will want to use your judgment in how you will apply this new feeling in taking action in the real

world, but you can use this technique to transform your feelings of powerlessness and despair.

Active Approaches to Transforming Helplessness

As noted above, you can also prevent depression by becoming an advocate for your child and trying to create change in her existing environments. If these approaches don't work, you can seek out alternative environments that support your vision of your child as gifted. Throughout this book, and specifically in chapter 4, we discussed strategies for becoming an advocate and not an apologist for your child. In chapter 9, it was suggested that you might even need to become a social activist in advocating for educational reform to meet your child's needs. If this approach is not your style, you can consider another approach for getting your child's needs met: finding alternative environments.

ALTERNATIVE MENTAL-HEALTH TREATMENT OPTIONS

Because some people might consider behavioral health interventions themselves to be alternative health options, this section will clarify a continuum of alternatives to medication for ADHD symptoms.

Review of the Standard Treatment Approach

According to the most current research on ADHD, the best approach to alleviating symptoms, including poor academic performance and family relations, is to combine medication and intensive behavior therapy (MTA Cooperative Group 1999). The standard treatment for ADHD is to see a pediatrician or a child psychiatrist who prescribes medication and monitors its dosage and effects on a regular basis. This standard treatment clearly defines and is defined by the medical model. As described in the introduction and first chapter, those who embrace the medical model understand ADHD as a brain dysfunction and treat it through medication intended to correct an organic, biologically based disorder.

As described in chapter 1, treating ADHD with medication has costs and benefits. The benefit is that research has shown that it is the most effective treatment for quickly reducing symptoms of ADHD in children. Among the many drawbacks of medications is the concern that there is no research on their long-term effects on children. Additionally, methylphenidate, one of the medications widely used to treat ADHD, is classified by the Drug Enforcement Agency as a Schedule II drug. Cocaine and morphine are also so classified, suggesting that these medications have a serious potential for becoming drugs of addiction.

Alternative Approaches

Alternative treatments for ADHD have increasingly become available. As a parent, these resources offer a great deal of hope and can be used in addition to or in place of medication, if appropriate. The increase of resources may also make your job more difficult, as you have to consider the time, money, and energy it requires to get access to them. Unfortunately, the research on ADHD treatments is not strong enough to offer clear recommendations based only on the empirical evidence. As an example of the primitive state of the field, the research on ADHD medications has not even extended into long-term studies of the safety and efficacy of this standard treatment. Given that the research is not extensive on even the standard medical treatment, there is even less research on alternative treatments.

If you're interested in finding approaches in addition to or in place of medication, the best strategy is to use treatments that have some empirical support and that have no evidence of potential negative effects. Given this standard, finding a psychotherapist who will support your child in applying cognitive behavioral interventions and supportive counseling would be helpful. Also, a recent treatment has been developed that has some preliminary research support for its effectiveness in helping children with ADHD in school settings. This treatment—neurofeedback—shows promise in changing actual brain functioning and has not had any documented negative side effects. While these adjunctive treatments may require resources, some parents have realized that without early intervention their child may not gain the skills needed to get into college and have thus justified using savings for college to pay for treatment for their children.

Confirm the Diagnosis

However, before launching into a full-scale effort at using every treatment available, a first step would be to make sure you have at least a second opinion in confirming the diagnosis of ADHD. Research has shown that the first suggestion of ADHD usually comes from teachers (Sax and Kautz 2003). Teachers' perceptions may be influenced by their own overburdened jobs, too many students in classes, and access to too few resources. Sometimes pediatricians and psychiatrists rely on the referral of parents and teachers without conducting a thorough assessment. Because the symptoms of ADHD overlap extensively with normal developmental behaviors, it is important that a thorough assessment be conducted in arriving at a diagnosis of ADHD. The diagnosis of ADHD requires a full range of symptoms present in more than one setting and usually entails checklists being filled out by both teachers and parents. A child can be disruptive in class and not meet the full criteria for ADHD. In this case, she should not be treated for the disorder by medication. Before expending time and energy treating ADHD, take the preliminary steps of confirming the diagnosis through a psychiatrist or psychologist trained in thorough assessment of this particular disorder.

Other Causes of ADHD-Like Symptoms

Children can show ADHD-like symptoms for many reasons other than having the actual disorder. For example, children may be disruptive because they are under too much stress. There may be family problems that they are acting out at school. Children who have suffered a recent loss (a parent, a grandparent, or sibling dying or having a serious health problem) can be expected to show disturbance in their behavior. These disruptions are usually reactions to life events and will pass if the child is given a chance to talk about and receive support for her concerns. A child may show ADHD-like symptoms because one parent is depressed or because there is serious marital conflict between her parents.

If your child did not have long-standing patterns of hyperactivity and attention problems but developed symptoms more suddenly, you should suspect some reaction to life events. You should ask yourself what major life events had recently occurred in your family prior to the appearance of ADHD-like symptoms. If you answer yes to any of the following questions, and your child's behavioral problems seemed to develop suddenly rather than being present for as long as you can remember, you might want to consider that your child does not have ADHD at all. Ask yourself the following questions:

- Did a parent lose a job?

- Has your child had health problems?

- Have there been health problems in family members?

- Have there been any deaths in the family?

- Have there been serious marital conflicts?

- Have any older siblings left the home?

- Has there been any physical, emotional, or sexual abuse?

- Is either parent depressed or anxious?

- Are there legal problems in the family?

- Are there serious financial problems in the family?

- Does either parent use or abuse alcohol or drugs?

Children are dramatically affected by these events, and it is predictable that their behavior will change to act out their fears, losses, anger, and stress. If children are given an opportunity to fully talk through their concerns and get support, you would expect dramatic improvements in behavior without formal treatment. If you answered yes to any of these questions, then the appropriate treatment would be a form of supportive treatment. Your child will need to learn to talk through her fears, anxieties, and doubts.

In place of or in addition to supportive therapy, the most effective way of handling reality-based distress of your child is to stay connected to her and offer to talk with her about her concerns. The more you can allow her feelings, contain them, offer her honest feedback, and reassure her as much as possible, the more she will be able to tolerate life stressors.

If the problems your child is reacting to are deep-seated family conflicts, then you should seek family therapy for the whole family or marital therapy for you and your partner. If one parent is suffering from depression or another mental-health disorder, including the use and abuse of drugs or alcohol, then that parent should seek individual treatment for the problem.

If these root problems are not addressed and your child is given medication to control her symptoms without getting necessary support, she may be at risk for long-standing behavioral problems. One reason for this is that she may never learn how to tolerate and work through the existential complications of life. If, as a parent, you recognize that one or more of the stressors listed above are present, you don't need to feel guilty or that you're to blame. Family problems are a perennial fact of life. You are not bad if you are depressed or have serious conflict with your spouse. Marital conflict, depression, anxiety, and professional setbacks can be expected to occur in any human life. Your child needs to be exposed to these difficulties and needs to receive support in dealing with them. You can think of this process as being similar to the way your child developed her immune system. Every child needs to be exposed to illness, get sick, and fight it off in order to develop a strong immune system. Similarly, you cannot just protect your child from life's trials and tribulations. The more she can work through her feelings and learn how to cope with difficult life events the more she will be prepared to cope with her own challenges as she grows more independent.

It is important that you review the stressors in your family and determine if and how much your child's symptoms are connected to a reaction to these stressors. As concluded by one alternative thinker, "Suppressing these symptoms by 'subduing' the child with medication hides from all the source of the child's troubles, precludes his being able to obtain mastery of his troubles through understanding, and subjects him to a false label of brain pathology" (Furman 2002, 141).

Neurofeedback

If you have confirmed a diagnosis of ADHD by a thorough assessment and have taken steps to address underlying reality-based causes of distress, you might take advantage of neurofeedback. This is a promising new intervention that works directly on training your child's brain to concentrate and focus. This procedure allows children, through exercises similar to video games, to practice gaining control over their attention and concentration. Because this is a newly emerging technology, it has not yet gained widespread acceptance. The procedure has not shown any negative side effects, and preliminary research studies demonstrate its effectiveness with individuals with ADHD.

The procedure of neurofeedback is similar to exercising the brain's attentional and control capacities through practice. Individuals get hooked up to monitors that provide feedback on what their brain is doing—concentrating or drifting off. As children learn to become aware of when they are gaining attentional control and are rewarded for this, they strengthen their capacity to focus. They also increase their capacity to identify when they are drifting off and can bring to bear their newfound skills to take control and pay attention.

Just as relaxation can be taught and trained, so can concentration. But in some ways, learning to concentrate is the opposite of learning to relax. Whereas relaxation entails a diffuse focus and a calm, passive attitude, concentration requires sharp focus, alertness, and active engagement with the world. Both of these ways of being can be trained. Children with ADHD need to learn to focus, just as a type A, high-pressured executive needs to learn to relax. Neurofeedback can help

The actual process of neurofeedback training requires a child to go to a clinic where she practices computer games that can only be played by controlling her concentration. Just as an athlete goes to the gym to increase her flexibility and strength, a child diagnosed with ADHD goes to a clinic to increase her attention and impulse control. The computer games are designed so that the child is rewarded for increased attention and focus. The child's brain wave patterns, as measured for an electroencephalogram (EEG), are used to measure the child's level of concentration.

Generally, the slower a child's brain waves, the more dreamy and unfocused she is, and the faster a child's brain waves, the more alert, focused, and in control she is. By getting continual feedback on her brain waves and getting rewarded by the video game for staying focused, the child learns to gain control over her mental state. When individuals are trying to relax, they are effectively training their brains to slow down their brain waves. In contrast, training a child with ADHD to focus means she learns to speed up her brain waves.

Generally, training in neurofeedback requires twenty to fifty visits to a neurofeedback clinic. While prices will likely vary by geographical region, a parent might expect to pay two thousand to five thousand dollars for a complete treatment. Emerging research provides preliminary evidence that neurofeedback is effective in reducing symptoms of ADHD. One study also reported increases in IQ scores of nineteen points, which is a dramatic and clinically meaningful improvement (Othmer, Othmer, and Kaiser 1999). Although most research on neurofeedback so far has studied small groups with no control conditions, there is emerging evidence that children experience improvements in school functioning after treatment and that these gains are long lasting (Lubar 1995). One of the most recent studies did include a large sample size (1,089 subjects from thirty-two clinics) and found improvement in attentiveness and impulse control following neurofeedback training (Kaiser and Othmer 2000).

One parent justified the cost of neurofeedback by reasoning that if he didn't get the help his child needed now, she wouldn't be able to attend college. The parent used college savings to finance the neurofeedback training. Anecdotally, children report enjoying the neurofeedback training. The actual training involves playing computer games and challenges children by teaching them how to control their minds. The assessment part of neurofeedback training involves having sensors placed on the child's head, and evokes a mysterious science fiction–like process where they can often see their own brain waves and electronic maps of their brain functioning.

Thus, a child with ADHD may be more open to neurofeedback than to going to a psychotherapist to talk about her feelings or to be trained to discipline her behavior. Neurofeedback directly impacts a child's capacity for control and concentration and has been shown to improve school performance dramatically. Anecdotally, other improvements in behavior and mood have been reported. One common report of benefits from neurofeedback is the "clean windshield effect." Individuals who have ADHD and others report feeling like the training has induced a state of mental and emotional clarity, almost as though they'd put on the windshield wipers and cleaned off a foggy, dirty windshield through which they view the world.

Neurofeedback resources. Resources for finding a neurofeedback training clinic are listed below:

- The Association for Applied Psychophysiology
  and Biofeedback
  303-422-8436
  www.aapb.org

- EEG Info
  www.eeginfo.com

- Brian Othmer Foundation
  818-373-1334
  www.brianothmerfoundation.org

- Southeastern Biofeedback and Neurobehavioral Institute
  865-584-8857
  www.eegfeedback.org

Also available are biofeedback training games for helping to regulate emotions. These resources don't qualify as neurofeedback because they do not track brain waves, concentrating instead on biological markers such as heart rate, respiration, and electrical skin responses. Two resources for biofeedback games you can buy and use on your computer are listed below:

- Freeze-Framer Emotional Management Enhancer
  800-372-3100
  www.heartmath.com

- The Wild Divine Project
  866-594-9453
  www.wilddivine.com

ALTERNATIVE EDUCATIONAL OPTIONS

In addition to exploring alternative mental-health treatment options, there are educational alternatives that may help in transforming your child. Statistically, children with ADHD will have many failure experiences in educational settings, including a 33 percent chance of being held back one year in school, with up to 35 percent of children so diagnosed failing to complete high school (Barkley 2000). While there is little conclusive and consistent research on how the environment in school settings impacts outcome, one leading researcher, Russell Barkley, outlines certain features of an educational setting that are likely to lead to positive outcomes for your child. His summarized conclusions are below:

- Positive outcomes are more likely if you increase novelty and stimulation, including color, shape, and texture to enhance attention and increase performance.

- Tasks should be of high interest to the child and active rather than passive. According to Barkley, "Tasks requiring an active as opposed to a passive response may also allow children with ADHD to better channel their disruptive behaviors into constructive responses" (236).

- Brief lessons with the child as an active participant will increase persistence.

- Include physical exercise to increase attention span.

- Positive outcomes are more likely if you include hands-on direct-instruction materials, like computers with software, that promote content learning

To the extent that you can advocate for these changes in your child's current educational system, you will be helping your child (as well as becoming a social activist). As noted in chapter 9, these changes are similar to those advocated by educational scholars who argue that the current educational system does not meet the needs of children who are growing up in the digital age rather than a culture dominated by modes developed during the industrial revolution.

There are alternative private educational settings that emphasize these forms of teaching and that are most consonant with the needs of a child diagnosed with ADHD. But it's not always true that the most expensive private schools will be the best match for your child. For example, many private college-preparatory schools will emphasize discipline, achievement, and a form of education least suited to the needs of a child with ADHD. In contrast, some independent private schools, advocate for different styles of learning and emphasize the independence of the child. If you are looking at independent private schools, you will want to find schools that have a philosophy that is consistent with the key principles listed above, such as individualized attention to your child, high levels of activity, and relative emphasis on your child's independent learning.

The Montessori Method

In addition to researching the philosophies of independent schools, you can look into schools with certain brand-name instructional methods. One example of a teaching method that seems ideally suited to children with ADHD is the Montessori method (Montessori 1967, 1966). All of the elements of an ideal educational setting listed by Barkley are fundamental to the Montessori method.

Individualized Lessons

The Montessori method uses individualized teaching methods rather than teaching a single lesson to a larger group. Maria Montessori writes that in an ideal teaching method, the teacher "will take care not to force a child's interest in what she is offering. If the lesson prepared with the necessary brevity, simplicity, and truth is not understood by the child as an explanation of the object, the teacher should be careful about two things. First, she should not insist on repeating the lesson. Second, she should refrain from letting the child know that he has make a mistake or has not understood, since this might arrest for a long time the impulse to act, which constitutes the whole basis for progress" (Montessori 1967, 107). As this quotation illustrates, the Montessori method is very different from standardized educational approaches. The methods are most suited to a child who needs individualized attention and gets easily lost in group lessons that require focused concentration on abstract concepts. In the Montessori method, the child chooses independent learning tasks based on her own needs and special interests.

Need for Physical Activity

Central to the Montessori method is the understanding that for children, learning requires physical movement. A child's mind is not yet fully rational and abstracted from her body, and it learns through action and moving in the world. Maria Montessori writes about physical activity, "Everybody admits that a child must be constantly on the move. This need for movement, which is irresistible in childhood, apparently diminishes with the development of inhibiting forces at the time when these, by entering into a harmony with the motor impulses, create the means for subjecting them to the will" (79). This emphasis on allowing children to move as they need and on sensory-based tasks that involve activity as a method for learning are ideally suited to the child diagnosed with ADHD. Note the commonsense notion that children have an internal need to be constantly in physical motion. While this idea may seem obvious, the current educational system defies this notion by requiring children to sit still to learn lessons. Also implicit in the Montessori method and the quotation above is that these methods of instruction may prevent the symptoms of ADHD from plaguing the life of a child. Maria Montessori seems to imply in this quotation and in other writings that if a child is allowed to learn through individualized attention and movement, she will internalize and develop the "inhibiting forces" that are the basis of discipline and concentration. Many authors have characterized ADHD as a failure to inhibit oneself. This line of reasoning leads to the radical and troubling possibility that some of the high rates of ADHD symptoms could be caused by educational methods that do not allow the full expression of the need to be physically active. If children are prohibited from the irresistible need for movement, they may not enter into "harmony with the motor impulses," which Montessori argues is the very means for "subjecting them to the will" and learning how to inhibit themselves.

Focus on Sensory Learning

One of the fundamental principles of the Montessori method is the emphasis on the child's engagement with the concrete, sensory world. There is little to no emphasis on grasping abstract knowledge. Rather, children in Montessori schools play and learn with concrete sensory objects of many different shapes and textures, not through standardized group lessons. For example, children play with movable letters of the alphabet manufactured in different textures to learn the fundamentals of reading. They can see the letters while also feeling their shapes and textures. At higher levels, children play with blocks to learn the fundamentals of algebraic manipulations. They move the blocks in conjunction with learning about numbers, adding, and subtracting.

Throughout this book, there has been a repeated emphasis on the need of a child with ADHD to learn through active engagement of her senses. As you can see, the Montessori method may be an appropriate match to this need. Again, there is also the suggestion that the lack of sensory education in standardized educational systems may play a causal role in creating ADHD-like symptoms. Maria Montessori writes, "[w]hen a fugitive mind fails to find something upon which it may work, it becomes absorbed with images and symbols. Children who are afflicted with this disorder move restlessly about. They are lively, irrepressible, but without purpose. They start something only to leave it unfinished, since their energies are directed toward many different objects without being able to settle upon any of them" (1966, 155). The implication is that if a child's inherent need to engage the sensory world is denied through emphasis on abstract learning, then symptoms of hyperactivity and difficulty in concentrating may result. Maria Montessori writes that if these symptoms have already developed, an education focused on direct sensory engagement with the environment and physical activity will lead to dramatic changes in the child's capacity for discipline and concentration.

In summary, the method of education your child receives can have a direct impact on her symptoms of ADHD. Maria Montessori's method suggests that the best education for any child is one that allows for individualized rather than group lessons, encourages physical activity, and focuses on sensory engagement with concrete objects rather than learning abstracted knowledge and facts. Her writing hints that if a child is denied these fundamental needs, symptoms that look like ADHD may develop.

Applying the Method

If you do not have access to a Montessori school, you can become an advocate for incorporating these elements of education into your child's current educational system. Additionally, you might want to incorporate your understanding of the inherent needs of children into your parenting style.

One simple adjustment you can make is to reframe your child's constant high levels of activity as representing an inherent need rather than disobedience. Maria Montessori's method suggests that children learn to inhibit behavior by connecting their mind and their body through active physical engagement with the environment. Thus, you may want to encourage and validate your child's need for constant movement. Some parents get frustrated with their child's need to touch and feel everything in the environment and see these behaviors as distractions from focused plans of activity. The more you can allow your child to engage with the environment in accord with her own interests, the more she will likely harmoniously connect her body and mind. The more words and abstract teaching she is subjected to, the more she experiences a disconnect between her mind and body. In some way, this takes a lot of pressure off of you as a parent. Rather than feeling that you have to provide knowledge to your child, you can shift your emphasis to permitting and allowing her exploration of her sensory environment. A child may benefit more from helping you make the bed than having you try to teach her the difference between a circle and a square through verbal instruction.

Summary

This chapter summarized the main principles for transforming your child. As you change your perception of your child from disordered to gifted and stay connected to your child, you will help her transform. This chapter also offered strategies for coping with the "real world," in which the perceptions of your child will not be informed by the new vision you have gained. Specific strategies were provided for interacting with the mental-health systems and educational systems in which your child participates.

References

Abram, D. 1996. *The Spell of the Sensuous*. New York: Pantheon Books.

American Psychiatric Association. 2000. *Diagnostic and Statistical Manual of Mental Disorders: Text Revision*. Washington, D.C.: American Psychiatric Association.

Arye, L. 2001. *Unintentional Music: Releasing Your Deepest Creativity*. Charlottesville, Va.: Hampton Roads.

Barkley, R. A. 2000. *Taking Charge of ADHD: The Complete Authoritative Guide for Parents*. New York: Guilford.

Breggin, P. R. 1991. *Toxic Psychiatry: Why Therapy, Empathy and Love Must Replace the Drugs, Electroshock and Biochemical Theories of the "New Psychiatry."* New York: St. Martin's Press.

Breggin, P. R., and D. Cohen. 1999. *Your Drug May Be Your Problem: How and Why to Stop Taking Psychiatric Medications*. Reading, Mass.: Perseus Books.

Faber-Taylor, A. F., F. E. Kuo, and W. C. Sullivan. 2001. Coping with ADD: The surprising connection to green play settings. *Environment and Behavior* 33:54-77.

———. 2002. Views of nature and self-discipline: Evidence from inner-city children. *Journal of Environmental Psychology* 22:49-63.

Franquemont, S. 1999. *You Already Know What to Do.* New York: Tarcher Putnam.

Freud, S. 1963. *Therapy and Technique.* New York: Collier.

Fulton, K. 1997. *Learning in a Digital Age: Insights into the Issues.* College Park, Md.: Center for Learning and Educational Technology, University of Maryland.

Furman, R. A. 2002. Attention deficit/hyperactivity disorder: An alternative viewpoint. *Journal of Infant, Child and Adolescent Psychotherapy* 2:125-144.

Giedd, J. N., J. Blumental, E. Molloy, and F. X. Castellanos. 2001. Brain imaging of attention deficit/hyperactivity disorder. In *Adult Attention Deficit Disorder: Brain Mechanisms and Life Outcomes,* edited by J. Wasserstein, L. E. Wolf, and F. F. Lefever. New York: New York Academy of Sciences.

Groth-Marnat, G. 2003. *Handbook of Psychological Assessment,* 4th ed. New York: Wiley.

Hartmann, T. 1997. *Attention Deficit Disorder: A Different Perception.* Grass Valley, Calif.: Underwood Books.

Hillman, J. 1983. *Healing Fiction.* New York: Station Hill.

Hillman, J., and M. Ventura. 1992. *We've Had a Hundred Years of Psychotherapy and the World's Getting Worse.* New York: Harper Collins.

Honos-Webb, L., Sunwolf, and J. L. Shapiro. 2001. Toward the re-enchantment of psychotherapy: stories as container. *The Humanistic Psychologist* 29:70-97.

Hoza, B., W. E. Pelham, D. A. Waschbusch, H. Kipp, and J. S. Owens. 2001. Academic task persistence of normally achieving ADHD and control boys: Performance, self-evaluations, and attributions. *Journal of Consulting and Clinical Psychology* 69:271-283.

Kaiser, D. A., and S. Othmer. 2000. Effect of neurofeedback on variables of attention in a large multi-center trial. *Journal of Neurotherapy* 4:5-15.

Kane, R., C. Mikalac, S. Benjamin, and R. A. Barkley. 1990. Assessment and treatment of adults with ADHD. In *ADHD: A Handbook for Diagnosis and Treatment*, edited by R. A. Barkley. New York: Guilford.

Leitner, L. M., A. J. Faidley, and M. A. Celentana. 2000. Diagnosing human meaning making: An experiential constructivist approach. In *Constructions of Disorder: Meaning-Making Frameworks for Psychotherapy*, edited by R. A. Neimeyer and J. D. Raskin. Washington D.C.: American Psychological Association.

Leo, J., and D. Cohen. 2003. Broken brains or flawed studies? A critical review of ADHD neuroimaging research. *The Journal of Mind and Behavior* 24:29-56.

Lubar, J. F. 1995. Neurofeedback for the management of attention-deficit/hyperactivity disorders. In *Biofeedback, A Practitioner's Guide*, edited by M. S. Schwartz et al. New York: Guilford.

Mahrer, A. R. 2004. *The Complete Guide to Experiential Psychotherapy.* Boulder, Colo.: Bull Publishing Company.

Migden, S. 2002. Self-esteem and depression in adolescents with specific learning disability. *Journal of Infant, Child and Adolescent Psychotherapy* 2:145-160.

Montessori, M. 1966. *The Secret of Childhood.* New York: Ballentine.

———. 1967. *The Discovery of the Child.* New York: Ballantine.

Mooney, J., and D. Cole. 2000. *Learning Outside the Lines.* New York: Fireside.

MTA Cooperative Group. 1999. A 14-month randomized clinical trial of treatment strategies for attention-deficit/hyperactivity disorder. *Archives of General Psychiatry* 56:1073-1086.

Nadis, S. 2004. In the line of fire. *Astronomy*, January.

Othmer, S., S. F. Othmer, and D. A. Kaiser. 1999. EEG biofeedback: An emerging model for its global efficacy. In *Introduction to Quantitative EEG and Neurofeedback*, edited by J. Evans and A. Abarbanel. San Diego, Calif.: Academic Press.

Owens, E. B., et al. 2003. Which treatment for whom for ADHD? Moderators of treatment response in the MTA. *Journal of Consulting and Clinical Psychology* 71:540-552.

Owens, J. S., and B. Hoza. 2003. The role of inattention and hyperactivity/impulsivity in the positive illusory bias. *Journal of Consulting and Clinical Psychology* 71:680-691.

Psychological Corporation. 1997. *WAIS-III/WMS-III Technical Manual*. San Antonio, Tex.: Psychological Corporation.

Rosenthal, R. 1987. Pygmalian effects: Existence, magnitude, and social importance. *Educational Researcher* 16:37-41.

Sax, L., and K. J. Kautz. 2003. Who first suggests the diagnosis of Attention-Deficit/Hyperactivity Disorder? *Annals of Family Medicine* 1:171-174.

Schultz, M. 1999. *Awakening Intuition: Using Your Mind-Body Network for Insight and Healing*. New York: Three Rivers Press.

Stein, D. B. 1999. *Ritalin Is Not the Answer: A Drug-Free, Practical Program for Children Diagnosed with ADD or ADHD*. San Francisco: Jossey-Bass.

VanKuiken, D. A. 2004. Meta-analysis of the effect of guided imagery practice on outcomes. *Journal of Holistic Nursing* 22:164-179.

Lara Honos-Webb, Ph.D., is a licensed clinical psychologist. She is the author of more than twenty publications in professional psychology journals and books. She is currently an assistant professor in the Counseling Psychology Program at Santa Clara University in Santa Clara, CA: She has presented her research both nationally and internationally. She is actively involved in the American Psychological Association.

Some Other
New Harbinger Titles

The Courage to Trust, Item 3805 $14.95

The Gift of ADHD, Item 3899 $14.95

The Power of Two Workbook, Item 3341 $19.95

Adult Children of Divorce, Item 3368 $14.95

Fifty Great Tips, Tricks, and Techniques to Connect with Your Teen, Item 3597 $10.95

Helping Your Child with OCD, Item 3325 $19.95

Helping Your Depressed Child, Item 3228 $14.95

The Couples's Guide to Love and Money, Item 3112 $18.95

50 Wonderful Ways to be a Single-Parent Family, Item 3082 $12.95

Caring for Your Grieving Child, Item 3066 $14.95

Helping Your Child Overcome an Eating Disorder, Item 3104 $16.95

Helping Your Angry Child, Item 3120 $17.95

The Stepparent's Survival Guide, Item 3058 $17.95

Drugs and Your Kid, Item 3015 $15.95

The Daughter-In-Law's Survival Guide, Item 2817 $12.95

Whose Life Is It Anyway?, Item 2892 $14.95

It Happened to Me, Item 2795 $17.95

Act it Out, Item 2906 $19.95

Parenting Your Older Adopted Child, Item 2841 $16.95

Boy Talk, Item 271X $14.95

Talking to Alzheimer's, Item 2701 $12.95

Helping a Child with Nonverbal Learning Disorder or Asperger's Syndrome, Item 2779 $14.95

The 50 Best Ways to Simplify Your Life, Item 2558 $11.95

Call **toll free, 1-800-748-6273,** or log on to our online bookstore at **www.newharbinger.com** to order. Have your Visa or Mastercard number ready. Or send a check for the titles you want to New Harbinger Publications, Inc., 5674 Shattuck Ave., Oakland, CA 94609. Include $4.50 for the first book and 75¢ for each additional book, to cover shipping and handling. (California residents please include appropriate sales tax.) Allow two to five weeks for delivery.

Prices subject to change without notice.